A MORE ARDENT FIRE

✷

To rise above self-centered desires, we require a more ardent desire and a nobler love – that of the Bridegroom. Finding delight and strength in Him, the soul gains the vigor and confidence it needs to abandon easily all selfish attachments . . .

—ST. JOHN OF THE CROSS

DATE DUE

OC 16 '03			
NO 12 '04			
JE 13 '07			
7-11-07			

A More Ardent Fire

FROM EVERYDAY LOVE TO LOVE OF GOD

by Eknath Easwaran

NILGIRI PRESS

I S B N : *cloth, 1–888314–03–6; paper, 1–888314–02–8*

First Printing May 2000

V02

The Blue Mountain Center of Meditation,

founded in Berkeley in 1960 by Eknath Easwaran,

publishes books on how to lead the spiritual life

in the home and the community.

For information please write to

Nilgiri Press, Box 256,

Tomales, California 94971

Web: www.nilgiri.org

Much of the material in this book

first appeared in the author's

Like a Thousand Suns.

Library of Congress Catalog Number: 00-103732

Table of Contents

Introduction

MANY YEARS AGO, after Mother Teresa achieved world recognition for her work in India, she came to visit the West. It wasn't long before she delivered a surprise: she had decided to extend her work to the United States, starting missions in New York and elsewhere – including, eventually, San Francisco.

By now we are used to seeing the Sisters of Charity with their white, blue-bordered saris in our streets. But at the time, the Bay Area met Mother Teresa's announcement with shock. After all, this was Mother Teresa of *Calcutta*, not San Francisco. We knew the third world needed her, but this was the first world, and San Francisco was the richest city in the richest state in the richest country on earth. What could someone like Mother Teresa have seen here that warranted placing it in the same category as Delhi, Colombo, and Addis Ababa?

I have never forgotten the answer she gave. "There is hunger for ordinary bread," she explained, "and there is hunger for love, for kindness, for thoughtfulness; and this is the great poverty that makes people suffer so much."

Coming from someone whose life was dedicated to "the lowest, the lowliest and the lost," those words went deep into my heart. Mother Teresa, who lived every day with people who were dying of hunger, was telling us that our own neighbors were starving too – starving for love.

In every human being, she was reminding us, there is a deep need for love – not only to be loved, but to give love as well. This need is written in our hearts. It is part of what we are as human beings, an inner necessity every bit as real as our need for food and drink. When we are deprived of it, we begin to die inside.

All the world's great religions explain this in the same way. We need to love, they tell us, because love is our real nature. "The soul is made of love," says Mechthild of Magdeburg, "and must ever strive to return to love. Therefore, it can never find rest nor happiness in other things. It must lose itself in love."

Once we grasp the sense of these quiet state-
ments, they can change our lives forever. They
mean that being able to love fully, unconditionally,
is our native state. We cannot lose this native capacity, cannot get rid of it even if we try. The most we
can manage to do is cut ourselves off from it, bury-
ing our capacity for love under layer after layer of
the self-centered conditioning that accumulates so
easily in the modern world. But that conditioning
can be removed, and when it is removed, what
remains is our original goodness – a capacity for
love that is, in principle, without limit.

At bottom, the promise of every personal relationship is to open up this wellspring of love deep
in our hearts. We aren't often aware of this promise,
of course. We think of love as an emotional or even
biochemical need that can be satisfied by something outside us. But it is a need to give, not to get.
And as Mechthild says, it is a need of the soul rather
than of the body – of our inmost self.

In other words, our hunger for love is really
spiritual.

And here we are in for a surprise. Despite what
the mass media assure us, if we want to learn about
love – even romantic love – we need to go to those

who really understand it: to Mother Teresa and Francis of Assisi, to Jesus and Mechthild and the Compassionate Buddha, to the luminous spiritual figures of every age and every culture who know that love is nothing casual or superficial but the very essence of who we are.

These luminous figures are the world's great mystics. This word *mystic* is one of the most misunderstood words I have ever encountered. It has been misused so often that we think mystics are people who turn their backs on life and isolate themselves from others in the search for a private, inner reality, "forgetting the world and by the world forgotten." Nothing could be further from the truth.

Experts tell us that very few people understand quantum dynamics. I would say even fewer understand spiritual dynamics. The spiritual life rests on four pillars:

First, underlying the ever-changing phenomena both around and within us lies a changeless reality that most major religions call God.

Second, this changeless reality is to be found not outside us but at the very core of our consciousness. There is a spark of divinity within us – in the soul, if you like, or, in Sanskrit, simply *atman,* the Self – that is not separate from God. The Sufi mystics put it beautifully: God is nearer to us than our body, dearer than our very life.

Third, this reality can be realized – uncovered and integrated into our character, consciousness, and conduct – by practices that are essentially the same in every religious tradition.

Finally, as every mystic will assure us passionately, this realization is the real purpose of life. It is possible to discover and base our daily lives on this changeless foundation. Nothing else can truly satisfy us. Far from being an otherworldly activity, living in the awareness of God is the most practical goal a human being can pursue. It brings happiness, meaning, and fulfillment where other satisfactions come and go.

But how are we to do this?

Here, I admit, traditional answers may not be helpful for most of us today. In every major religion, the search for this changeless reality has often led to a life of withdrawal from the rest of the world. I have profound respect for this path, but very few of us are capable of or even desire a cloistered life. We want a way to pursue a spiritual life in the context of close, personal relationships with family and friends. We want, in short, what the world's religions call the Way of Love.

One of the worst misconceptions about the spiritual life is that we have to drop out of the world to pursue it – turn our back upon our family, go away from society, get into a cave, and sit there for twelve years until illumination dawns. In my eyes, the spiritual life is one of selfless action and rich relationships with everyone around, extending not merely to a few among family or friends, but wider and wider until our love embraces the whole of life.

In India, where religion has been regarded for thousands of years as an art, a skill, and even a science, there is a little manual on the Way of Love that would be recognized by mystics everywhere because it is so free from dogma. It is embedded in the Bhagavad Gita, India's best-loved scripture. Like parts of the *Imitation of Christ,* it is composed as a dialogue between the human and the divine – between Arjuna, a warrior prince who represents you and me, and Sri Krishna, an incarnation of the Lord. "What is the best path to you," Arjuna asks, "the Way of Knowing or the Way of Love?" The reply is so practical and so inspiring that I have laid out this book as a commentary on each verse, drawing on my own experience to illustrate the applications to everyday life.

The implication of this teaching is simple but very far reaching. Love is a skill that every one of us can learn – not merely for personal enrichment, but so that deepening and strengthening our relationships becomes a sure, swift path toward making God a reality in our daily lives.

There is really no end to which this love can grow. Just as when you stand on Mount Everest and look around, you are overwhelmed by the beauty of creation, similarly, when you scale these dizzy heights of the superconscious and look around, you will be overwhelmed to see the whole world shining with unity – sky and sea, mountains and rivers, forests and lakes and creatures great and small, all as expressions of one unbroken whole. The joy that comes with this vision cannot be put into words. The love that flows through your heart then will make you want to exclaim with Francis of Assisi, "Any more and my very life would melt away!"

Meditation

The tool for scaling these lofty heights of the spirit is meditation. What we are really trying to do in meditation is to remove the innumerable obstacles that hide and cover our native capacity for love, until in the end we not merely love, but we become love itself. When this happens, we see the same divine presence simultaneously in the hearts of everyone, regardless of who they are or how they conduct themselves towards us. Race, color, gender, nationality, have no more significance than the color of a person's jacket. All barriers fall; all separateness is gone. Everyone's joy becomes your joy; everyone's welfare is inseparable from your own. That is what love means; that is the capacity already present in your heart. And for releasing this capacity for love, there is nothing on earth like meditation.

This book was taken from talks I gave as a teacher of meditation to some of my closest students, so I refer often to the method of meditation I teach – the same method I have followed myself for over half a century. This method fits naturally into any religious outlook, for it consists in going slowly, in the mind, through words from a great scripture or mystic, giving each word or phrase one's fullest attention and bringing the mind back whenever it wanders. Since the passages are chosen for their appeal to one's own highest ideals, daily meditation on them gradually brings those ideals to life in thought and action.

As you can see, this is identical with practices called by other names in other traditions – interior prayer, contemplation, prayer of the heart. But whatever it is called, meditation is training the mind – teaching your thoughts and desires to obey you. As you practice, this deceptively simple skill of training your mind will gradually enable you to withdraw your attention when it wanders to negative thoughts and actions, to compulsive habits and states of mind. The passages you choose for meditation represent your highest ideals. They remind you of the kind of person you would like to become. When you meditate on them every day with sustained attention, you drive them deep into your consciousness, where they will begin to prompt your thought and action during the day.

To strengthen this link between meditation and daily life, I teach meditation as one point of an eight-point program:

1. *Meditation*
2. *The Mantram or Holy Name*
3. *Slowing Down*
4. *One-Pointed Attention*
5. *Training the Senses*
6. *Putting Others First*
7. *Spiritual Companionship*
8. *Reading the Mystics*

One of these points that needs a little extra introduction is the use of what in India is called a *mantram:* a sacred phrase or name of God. This, too, is a practice found in every mystical tradition I know of. I ask my students to choose a mantram that appeals to them deeply, selected from those established by long tradition (I have given a list on page 223–224). Then I ask them to use it throughout the day whenever they are doing something that does not require attention, such as waiting in a queue or taking a walk. Like meditation, this is a way of training attention – an extremely power-ful way, as you will find when you try it. When you feel yourself getting angry or agitated, for exam-ple, go out for a brisk walk repeating the mantram. *Jesus, Jesus* or *Ave Maria, Barukh attah Adonai* or *Rama, Rama* – whichever it is, the Holy Name will calm your mind and quietly remind you of the lofty purpose for which you chose it.

There is a brief but adequate set of instructions for following all these eight points at the end of this book for those who would like to experiment with this program, or who want a better grasp of the practices I talk about in the following chapters.

Over the years I have often had people come up after a talk and tell me, "This sounds great, but I'm just not capable of the kind of selfless love you talk about. I get jealous easily; I get resentful; I can be awfully self-willed. I don't really want to accept this about myself, but I don't know what to do about it. I think I'm just not capable of love."

I always reply, "All of us have to learn to love, just as we had to learn to walk or speak. But every one of us *can* learn, and I have never met anyone who couldn't learn to love more."

This is where meditation shines as a tool with truly limitless power. Through the practice of meditation, if you give it your very best every day, you can change your personality completely – from selfish to unselfish, from insecure to secure, from unloving to loving, from separate into whole.

PART ONE

The Way of Love

1 *O Lord, of those who love you as*
the Lord of Love, ever present in
all, and those who seek you as the
nameless, formless Reality, which
way is sure and swift, love or
knowledge?

IN EVERY RELIGION, the mystics speak broadly of two paths to God: the Way of Knowing and the Way of Love. This little book begins with a very natural question: "Which is best? What path shall I follow?"

This simple question has far-reaching implications, for it involves a very basic issue: what are we, as human beings, and what can we become? Are we merely physical creatures, who can be satisWed with physical things and experiences, or are we something more? And not only what do we say we believe, but how do we actually live?

These are not theoretical questions. They affect every aspect of our lives. Our upbringing, our

relationships, our attitude toward the environment, our physical and emotional well-being are
all conditioned by the assumption that the basis
of the human being is physical. Even personality
is considered to be a product of our genetic makeup. Deep in our consciousness, whether we think
about it or not, this is the picture to which all of us
subscribe: character is something we are born with,
and we have little choice but to accept ourselves the
way we are.

This belief has tragic consequences, for it limits
our outlook everywhere to the lowest common fac-
tor of existence. To borrow an image from William
James, believing we are merely physical creatures is
like going through life moving only our little finger.
We don't suspect that this finger is part of a much
larger whole; we think it is all we have.

Here I like to remember the example of Albert
Einstein, whose theories revolutionized the physical sciences. When he was asked how he discovered
relativity, Einstein replied simply, "By questioning
an established axiom." In the same way, the mystics
call into question our concept of the human personality, and therefore the basis of our civilization.

Their challenge is simple: we are not what our genes are; the body is. We are what we think. Behavior may be determined by our genetic makeup, but only in so far as we lack control over what we think. The promise of meditation is that it can enable us to get below the surface level of consciousness and begin to take control of the thinking process itself. Then we can go beyond conditioning and start to reshape our personality.

By its nature, science is limited to the physical world of finite objects and passing events. But this is just the surface of reality – only the part that our five senses can perceive in a framework of space and time. As Spinoza puts it, "The finite rests upon the bosom of the Infinite." Science investigates the infinite variety of the measurable world; spiritual insight looks into what sustains that world, from a vantage point beyond change.

It is the same with the human being. Here, too, with our physical orientation, we see only the surface – the body and its biochemistry – and mistake that for the whole. But there is much, much more. Roughly speaking, the mystics of all traditions present the same picture of personality.

The outermost wrapper is the body; but "within," no longer physical, lie the regions of the mind. Deeper still is the intellect or will. And innermost is the soul, with, as Meister Eckhart says, a "spark of the divine" at its very core. This model of personality is found throughout the annals of world mysticism, and in it, as you can see, the body is only the thinnest shell of who we are.

When we lose track of these worlds within us, we think of ourselves and everything else – including other people – as physical. Naturally, when we have a problem, we look for a physical solution. But very few of the important issues in life – those that threaten our health, our happiness, our relationships, our very survival – can be solved on the physical level. In such cases, trying to apply a physical solution is all too likely to make the problem more acute, because we are usually dealing not with the cause but with the symptoms.

Some years ago, for example, surgeons began to treat extreme cases of obesity by bypassing part of the intestine. It was, of course, a drastic measure, only undertaken under life-threatening circumstances. But the operating assumption was that nothing else remained to be done. From the mystic's perspective, it is important to remember that even when such measures are deemed necessary, they are superficial. It is always possible to go beneath the surface of consciousness and change the underlying pattern of compulsive thinking. If this is forgotten, medical and surgical interventions quickly become practiced in an isolated realm where nonphysical consequences are ignored.

This does not contradict the miraculous discoveries in biology that are laying bare the mechanics of life at the molecular level. It includes biology as part of a larger picture. But it *is* at odds with the belief that personality is genetically determined. I have seen textbooks comparing the genetic code to a movie film, unrolling through our lives. To the extent that we identify ourselves with the body and are subject to biological conditioning, this may be valid. But we are not what our DNA is. Genes may limit how tall we can be, but they can't limit the stature to which we can grow as human beings.

If our lives were a film, the genes would only be stage hands. The director is what I call ego: our self-centered, conditioned personality. The mind gets the supporting roles, and countless desires run about as extras to make up for the lack of plot. This is the first reel, and if we could see it clearly we would want our money back.

In meditation, however, we get hold of the camera and the direction. The supporting cast is the same, the makeup artist and set designer are the same, but we get a new script and a new star. Even biologically, we have become a different person: the genetic material is the same, but behavior is different, thinking is different, the person is wholly transformed. We can watch this transformation in the lives of great figures like Francis of Assisi, Teresa of Avila, Mahatma Gandhi, and countless others East and West who make an about-face that changes them completely. Then, as Meister Eckhart says, "The old man is dead and the new man is born; the pauper is dead and the prince is born."

2 THE LORD:

*For those who set their hearts
on me and worship me with
unfailing devotion and faith,
the Way of Love leads sure and
swift to me.*

IN INDIA there is a story about a villager who wanted to learn to meditate. For several weeks, following his teacher's instructions, he tried to fix his mind on the formless Absolute. But his mind did nothing but wander. Finally he went back to his teacher and complained, "Sir, I just can't keep my mind on the Absolute. I don't know what it's like."

The teacher got the hint and decided to take a more practical approach. "All right," he said, "what is it that appeals to you most deeply?"

With some embarrassment the villager replied, "My cow."

"Very well," said the teacher, "go and meditate on your cow." That is one of the skills of a good spiritual teacher; he always knows how to begin where you are.

A while later the teacher decided to look in on his new student. To his surprise, the man hadn't come out of his meditation room for days. His teacher pounded on the door. "Open up!" he commanded. "What are you doing in there?"

There came a faint answer, a little like a bellow: "Meditating."

"Come out at once," the teacher repeated. "I have some instructions to give you about moderation."

"Sir," came the reply, "I can't come out. My horns are too big to fit through the door."

This is the basis of meditation: we become what we meditate on. Whatever we constantly dwell on shapes our desires, our decisions, and finally our destiny. Put simply, we become what we love.

In this sense, every one of us has been meditating for a long time. The problem is that we have no control over what we meditate on.

To take a negative example, look at what happens over a period of years to someone whose love has been captured by money. At first he may show only a tendency to be greedy. But if he continues to dwell on making money, that desire begins to condition his ways of thinking. Making a profit comes easily to such a person, for the simple reason that he doesn't really see anything else. As the Buddha would remind us, we don't see with our eyes. We see with our mind, and here the mind is always thinking about money. When he visits a redwood grove, he sees a fortune in the lumber market. When he stands at the rim of the Grand Canyon at dawn, he thinks about damming up the river for a resort. And the tragedy is that after many years, he won't be able to think of anything else. He will be so preoccupied with profit that he won't be aware of the needs of family or friends or society. He may even be willing to work at jobs that are harmful to others, such as manufacturing cigarettes or selling armaments, simply to make a few more dollars. In a sense, it is no longer realistic to expect him to be otherwise; he just can't see any other way. This is the immense power of thoughts, which few of us even suspect.

But all this has a positive side too. Just as we stunt ourselves by dwelling on some private, personal satisfaction, we can grow to our full stature by giving our love to an ideal that embodies the perfection of human nature.

The annals of mysticism are full of examples of this, but I know of none more appealing, more human, than that of St. Francis of Assisi. He was born into a well-to-do merchant family, and though he must have been a sweet-tempered young man, his mind seems to have been full of no more than poetry and music and the romance of the Crusades. But when his heart turned to Jesus, his desire to become like him was so passionate that it transformed and transfigured him completely. As G. K. Chesterton has said, if you find the Jesus of the Gospels unapproachable, if you find it hard to believe that the Sermon on the Mount can actually be practiced by a human being, you have only to look at Francis, the perfect image of his Master.

If this is difficult to understand, it is because most of us have no idea of what love really means. Look at how the word *love* is used today, not only in the mass media but by some of the most respected people in every profession. It shows how unreal our world has become; everything is a matter of biology. If someone says, "Two people are embracing each other; they are making love," we consider that

an intelligent statement. But if I were to see someone being patient in the face of provocation and
say, "That person is making love," people would
think it was a quaint example of a professor from
India mixing up his English idioms. How thor-
oughly we have turned life upside down! What is
untrue is universally accepted, and what is true
cannot even be understood.

When I first came to this country, I gave a talk on
the spiritual life to a group of teenage girls. In those
days practically no one had heard of meditation, so
I centered my remarks around something in which
girls of that age are always interested: personal relationships. The young president of the club lis-
tened very carefully, and when I had finished she
said, "You have used the word *love* a lot, but not the
way we are used to hearing it. Will you please tell
us what love means to you?"

I like that kind of direct question very much, and
I told her: "When I say I love a person, it means only
one thing: that person's happiness, that person's
welfare, means more to me than my own."

She looked around at the others. "Well, girls," she
confessed, "I guess that means none of us has ever
been in love."

It was a thoughtful observation, for this is a concept of love that does not even occur to most of us today. To the mystics, love has very little to do with sentimental or physical attraction. I don't think anyone has described it better than St. Paul:

> Love suffers long, and is kind; love envies not; love vaunts not itself, is not puffed up, does not behave itself unseemly, seeks not its own, is not easily provoked, thinks no evil; rejoices not in iniquity, but rejoices in the truth; bears all things, believes all things, hopes all things, endures all things. Love never fails.

In the traditional interpretation, the Way of Love is a path toward love of God. But I don't think it is any exaggeration to say that its essence is simply to love. As St. John says, if we fail in love of others we cannot say we know God, for God is love. Even to love another person completely, our consciousness has to be united, which is the very essence of the spiritual life.

On this, mysticism East and West agree completely. All mystics would concur with St. Paul's eloquent exclamation: "Not I, not I, but Christ liveth in me." Lover and Beloved are one. And if we can cast our eyes to the summit of human nature, isn't it the same even between two individuals in love? What passes for love today is a kind of contract. "Here are my duties, here are yours. This is the boundary line. If you stay on your side, I'll respect you; but if you cross over, you're invading my space." Wherever people go their separate ways like this, there can be no love; there is scarcely a relationship. The very nature of love, whether human or divine, is not to have qualifications or reservations at all.

When the mystics talk like this people sometimes object, "I've never spent a day like that, much less a lifetime! If that's what love means, I don't think I'm capable of it." I have never accepted this statement from anybody. Every one of us can learn to love. Naturally, we all start with imperfections: rigidities, self-centered habits, demands and opinions of our own. But there is no need to throw up our hands as so many are doing today and say, "Let's be separate and have a relationship"; it is not possible to do both. Instead, we start where we are — somewhat selfish, somewhat self-centered, but with a deep desire to relate lovingly to each other, to move closer and closer together. It requires a lot of stamina and many years of hard work, and there will be anguish in it as well as joy. But there is one immediate consolation: we don't have to wait until our love is perfect to reap the benefits of it. Even with a little progress, everyone benefits – not only those we live with, but we ourselves as well.

This is the Way of Love the mystics present. It is not at all limited to romance, but a loving relationship between man and woman provides a particularly good context because the desire for union is already present. It needs only to be nurtured, so that every day you love each other a little more.

The Sufis have a vivid image to illustrate this. In some parts of Muslim society, it is still not uncommon to see women wearing the veil. I first saw this at close quarters when I was teaching on a campus in Central India, where the women students would sometimes sit together behind a common veil on one side of the room. This veil aroused great curiosity: all the boys wanted to see who was behind it. You could hear the girls' bangles jingling and now and then a soft ripple of laughter, and none of my best quotes from Shakespeare could compete with those delicate sounds.

At first the veil seemed opaque. But as I looked with more attention, I began to make out silhouettes behind it. Then I could see some of the features, and finally, as I learned what to look for, I was able to recognize the faces on the other side.

This is what happens in personal relationships on the path of love. At first there is a curtain between us and the one we love. The Lord is present there, but we cannot see him – in fact, at the beginning we scarcely know what to look for. Gradually, however, our concentration deepens. Now we sense that there really is someone behind the curtain, and every once in a while we glimpse a silhouette. As vision becomes clearer, we begin to see what Nicholas of Cusa called "the Face behind all faces" – and the more we see, the deeper is our desire to see more.

In the end, all our other desires merge in the immense longing to have no barrier between us and our real Beloved. Only one veil remains, and it is so thin that every morning we go to meditation with the passionate hope that this will be the day when we are united with the Lord at last. We may wait like this for years, but finally, without warning, the veil falls at last. Then, in the rapturous language of St. John of the Cross, we merge with the Beloved and are transformed: *"Amado con amada, amada en el amado transformada."*

Most of us think of love as a one-to-one relationship, which is all it can be on the physical level. But there is no limit to our capacity to love. We can never be satisfied by loving just one person here and another there. Our need is to love completely, universally, without any reservations – in other words, to become love itself. It can take our breath away to glimpse the vastness of such love, which Dostoevsky describes beautifully in *The Brothers Karamazov:*

> Love all that has been created by God, both the whole and every grain of sand. Love every leaf and every ray of light. Love the beasts and the birds, love the plants, love every separate fragment. If you love each separate fragment, you will understand the mystery of the whole resting in God. When you perceive this, your understanding of this mystery will grow from day to day until you come to love the whole world with a love that includes everything and excludes nothing.

This is what unconditional love means, and in these troubled times, when turmoil has invaded our society, our homes, and even our hearts, I don't think there is any more precious attainment. As one Hasidic rabbi put it, the community of the living is the carriage of the Lord. Where there is so little love that the carriage is torn asunder, we must love more: the less love there is around us, the more we need to love to make up the lack.

A man once came to the Ba'al Shem Tov and said, "My son is estranged from God; what shall I do?" The Ba'al Shem replied simply, "Love him more." This was Mahatma Gandhi's approach to every problem, and I know of no more effective or artistic or satisfying way to realize the unity of life in the world today. It is an approach to life in which everything blossoms, everything comes to fruition. To ask which way is better, love or knowledge, is really unnecessary. Where there is love, everything follows. To love is to know, to love is to act; all paths of self-realization are united in the way of love.

3 *As for those who seek the transcendental Reality, without name, without form, contemplating the Unmanifested, beyond the reach of thought and of feeling, with their senses subdued and mind serene and striving for the good of all beings — they too will verily come unto me.*

THIS IS the other concept of God: not a personal ideal that can be loved, but the formless, impersonal ground of existence. Many people subscribe to this idea today, in the belief that faith in a personal God is either superstition or intellectual weakness. But the impersonal Godhead has nothing to do with intellectual abstraction. The intellect can operate only in a world of duality, where subject is separate from object and knower from known. Here we must soar beyond all divisions into a realm of absolute unity, where the separate personality merges completely in this formless, infinite Reality and all distinction between knower and known disappears. In this supreme state there is no one present to take notes. Sri Ramakrishna, a great Indian saint from the nineteenth century, used to tell about a doll made of salt who went to measure the depth of the ocean. As soon as she waded into the water, she dissolved – and then, Ramakrishna asks, who was left to tell of the ocean's vastness?

In this realm all trace of distinction disappears, so it is not surprising that we find mystics of all epochs and all traditions struggling to describe their experience in much the same language. Meister Eckhart in thirteenth-century Germany and Shankara in eighth-century India often sound interchangeable; and Dionysius the Areopagite, probably a Christian monk writing at the end of the fifth century, uses terms reminiscent of this very verse:

> Then, beyond all distinction between knower
> and known, ... the aspirant becomes merged in
> the nameless, formless Reality, wholly absorbed
> in that which is beyond all things and in nothing
> else. . . . Having stilled his intellect and his mind,
> he is united by his highest faculty with that which
> is beyond all knowing.

To the intellect, which has to classify, the Way of Knowing and the Way of Love are watertight compartments. But in fact, they are not separate. They are different aspects of the same spiritual experience, which flow together in life and practice.

To see this, all we have to do is look at those men and women who have followed the Way of Knowing – not at their philosophy, but at their lives. Shankara, for example, is remembered as a towering intellectual, the architect of an imposing philosophical structure that expounds his direct experience of the transcendent, impersonal Godhead, "One without a second." But this same uncompromising nondualist was also an ardent lover of the personal God who poured out his devotion in magnificent poetry. He died at the age of thirty-two, but in that short lifetime he traveled all over India, tirelessly revitalizing its spiritual heritage – founding monastic orders, establishing monasteries, teaching successors, and leaving behind a great body of writing to pass on the fruit of his spiritual experience. In such a life, love, selfless service, and spiritual wisdom all merge; each path comes to perfection in the same soul.

The formless Godhead cannot be described, because there is nothing from which it can be distinguished. It is "what is and what is not," from which, as Shankara says, both "words and thought recoil." Still, to inspire us, this verse tries to convey a little of the stark majesty of this infinite, eternal Reality. It is inexhaustible, imperishable, without either beginning or end. We cannot point to it or define it because it is neither outside nor inside; subject and object are one. It cannot be seen. Who could be the seer? Yet it is everywhere; it is existence itself. It is unshakable, beyond all change.

These inspiring words give a glimpse of our real nature – the nature of the soul, of our real Self. We were never born; we shall never die. But at the same time, they give an idea of the awesome challenges of the Way of Knowing, which I do not hesitate to say is beyond the capacity of all but a handful of people in any age. It is very well to say "I am not my body, I am not my mind," but for most of us, how much effect would this have on behavior? We would still get angry, still harbor resentments, still be subject to doubt and vacillation. As long as it is only an intellectual effort, this sort of exercise has nothing to do with spiritual insight.

In the second half of this verse we get the qualifications required for traveling this lofty path to the Godhead. They are really stiff. First, there must be complete self-control. The senses do not clamor for anything, and if they do happen to ask timidly for something pleasant, we should be able to withdraw that desire without a hint of protest. The mind should be free from likes and dislikes and from any kind of personal entanglement. Our joy in life should lie in serving the welfare of others without any thought of personal satisfaction. To me, this is all very much like the escape clauses you find in small print on the back of a contract: "If you can follow this path, you don't need it; you are practically at your goal. And if you do need it, you won't be able to follow it."

In this connection, Sri Ramakrishna tells a story about the cowherd girls who were Sri Krishna's companions in his youth. In these stories these girls represent all of us, the aspiring human soul; and they are passionately in love with Sri Krishna, the Lord of Love.

One day, Ramakrishna says, a wandering sage passed through the village. Seeing that these girls were completely devoted to a personal form of

God, he decided to teach them about the imper-sonal Godhead. One by one, the girls fell asleep. When they woke up again they explained apologet-ically, "Holy one, we don't understand any of this. All we know about is our Krishna, whom we can see and enjoy and love."

Ask any young man whether he would rather have a date with Miss Principle of Femininity or with his girlfriend. Miss Femininity is perfect, but she is also formless – in fact, she doesn't have any attributes at all. If I know anything about men, that chap will tell you candidly to keep your Miss Perfection for yourself; he would rather go out with the girl he loves. She may have freckles and an unpredictable temper, but she has a hand he can hold, eyes he can gaze into, and a smile that lightens his heart.

Though we may pride ourselves on our intellect, it is the same with us when it comes to knowing God. Identifying ourselves with the body as we do, how is it possible to aspire to disembodied con-sciousness? It is not enough for the Lord to be eter-nal and immutable; he must also be packaged attractively in a human form. This is the miracle of divine incarnation, and when the Lord comes to life like this in a human being, it can capture our imagination and unify our love completely. As St. Bernard explains, "The main reason for the invisible God incarnating himself physically in the midst of human beings was to lead them who can only love physically to the healthy love of his physical appearance, and then, little by little, to spiritual love."

4 *Yet hazardous and slow is the path to the Unrevealed, difficult for physical beings to tread.*

THE WAY OF KNOWING, as an Indian mystic once summarized, "is for those whose senses have come under complete control."

That is the rub. For those who meet the qualifications – giants like Meister Eckhart or Shankara – the path of knowledge is a perfectly adequate vehicle for the spiritual life. These are people who are so free from the clamor of the senses that they scarcely identify with their bodies at all. But unless we know in our heart that we are not the body, as this verse says, we are going to find this path very tough going.

Unfortunately, there are very few in the world today who fall into this category. Virtually all of us believe that we are the body. If you doubt it, all you have to do is look around and ask a very simple question: How do we spend our time? When we want to celebrate, do we meditate or do we eat? When we get a vacation, what do we choose to do? What are the usual themes in the books and magazines we read, the songs we listen to, the movies and television shows we watch? We may protest, "This is the age of science. Knowing *has* to be the right path for us." But the mystics would only smile. "Do your senses obey you? If they do, you might be on the right track. But if they insist on getting what they want, you'd better consider the Way of Love instead."

This is not a comment on the effectiveness of the Way of Knowing. It is a comment on the physical conditioning with which all of us have grown up. Ours is a physically oriented world, so we should not be embarrassed to discover that we have learned to look on ourselves as physical creatures.

But we need not resign ourselves to this conditioning. We can change our way of thinking – and until we do, we are going to find it very difficult to maintain any lasting relationship with those around us. The fiercer our physical conditioning is, the more separate we will feel and the more we will be prey to all the problems of a divided mind: vacillation, depression, jealousy, and alienation. These problems can be solved, but not on the physical level where they arise. We need access to much deeper levels of consciousness.

Take, for example, a Don Juan who is all involved in a meaningful relationship with a young lady named Dulcinea. Juan is a very passionate fellow and intensely jealous. His mother will tell you that is his nature; he cannot change. Unfortunately, since Dulcinea is attractive, Juan's life is an agony of suspicion. The minute she is out of his sight he can't concentrate on anything, he can't enjoy anything, he can't stop worrying about what she is doing.

Now, according to one school of thought, the problem is this couple's "chemistry." Don Juan plus Dulcinea is a combination that is never going to work, because of how Juan is. Perhaps, if he can exchange his Dulcinea for a Juanita . . . But unfortunately, as most of us know from our own experience, this simply doesn't work. Juan has a jealous mind. He has to be jealous of somebody, and if Dulcinea is not around, he will be jealous of her maid. The problem is not with Dulcinea or Juanita or anything else in the outside world; the problem is the uncertainty in the mind of Juan. As long as he identifies himself physically, he cannot help being possessive; he will be at the mercy of his glands.

But it *is* possible for Juan to overcome his jealousy: not by reasoning with it, not by suppressing it, not by taking security hormones, but by learning to master his own mind. When that is done, all insecurity goes – not only insecurity over Dulcinea, but insecurity over anything. Then he can take Dulcinea out to the Alhambra café, where her former boyfriend plays flamenco, and not be apprehensive at all. Juan's face may look the same, his fingerprints may be the same, but Dulcinea will assure us that he has become a different person.

For years I have been following the research into what is called the "biochemical basis of personality." It is a fascinating field. Just as in our galaxy there are billions of stars, there is a galaxy in our heads: the ten billion cells of the human brain. When Galileo is looking through his telescope at the galaxy of stars, he is seeing them through this galaxy inside. And just as the Milky Way contains all kinds of worlds, each self-contained but part of an integral whole, there are biochemical island-worlds in the galaxy of the brain – the cerebral cortex, the hippocampus, the thalamus, the amygdala – each with its histories of growth and commerce in which whole dynasties of proteins rise and fall.

This is not merely figurative language. Just as it is all one universe, for all those countless billions of separate stars, it is all one person and not just a lot of brain cells.

Scientists have managed to probe deep into the molecular and genetic makeup of the brain. Among other things, they can trace neurotransmitters like dopamine and serotonin that trigger changes in mood. But if anyone suggests that by manipulating brain biochemistry we can elevate consciousness, we ought to raise our eyebrows. The brain is not conscious; it is an instrument of consciousness. When consciousness is changed, there will naturally be correlated changes in brain biochemistry and behavior. But by changing the biochemistry of the brain, we cannot change consciousness itself. All we can do is suppress particular symptoms, which is often like trying to solve an electrical problem in a car by removing the little red warning light on the dash.

Researchers, for example, have learned that certain tranquilizing drugs can have a quieting effect on people whose anxiety seems linked to their overactive behavior. Often these are people with uncontrollable energy – which, from a physical perspective, is a serious liability. From a spiritual perspective, however, this kind of behavior is often an expression of tremendous vital capacity which is crying out to be harnessed. Such people may have the potential for great achievements, and quieting their behavior with drugs, is going to suppress their capacity for achievement as well as their capacity for running amok. It is the same capacity: that is the key.

Of course there will be times when drugs are useful in controlling severe anxiety or depression. But this use must be carefully supervised and judicious. In sedation, what happens is that the medication blunts the cutting edge of consciousness. After some time of this, we don't even have the blade of consciousness any more; we have only the handle. This is one danger of manipulation on the physical level: it may bring temporary relief of symptoms, but it can also worsen the underlying problem.

The real issue with trying to manipulate personality like this is the damage to human growth. In every attempt at a physical or biochemical solution, the will is forgotten or even undermined – and without the will we have no capacity for choice, no capacity for growth, no capacity for love. That is what the biochemical approach to personality can lead to when it is taken to extremes. To release our real human potential we need to get to a deeper level of consciousness, where we can deepen our will and make the choices that enable us to grow.

5 *But they for whom I am the goal supreme, who do all work renouncing self for me and meditate on me with single-hearted devotion — these will I swiftly rescue from the fragment's cycle of birth and death to fullness of eternal life in me.*

WHEN MY WIFE and I were living on the Blue Mountain in India, we had a visit from a young American who had been living in the Himalayas for many years as a spiritual aspirant. He was dressed just like a traditional Indian mendicant, but when he spoke, his English still betrayed a Harvard accent.

We talked about the spiritual life for some time, and when evening came he offered to come with us to our little meditation center and give the inspirational talk. Our group consisted mostly of simple villagers, and I was afraid his words might be too sophisticated. But there was no cause for worry. He spoke their native Tamil without stumbling, and the story he told was one that anyone could understand.

"Look," he said, stretching out his hands with open palms. "Sri Krishna is saying to every one of us, 'Here, I have a very special gift for you: the gift of immortality. Won't you reach out and take it?'

"'Thank you,' we say, 'but can't you see? Our hands are already full with these sweet mangoes.'

"Sri Krishna smiles. 'Let go of the mangoes,' he explains patiently. 'Then your hands will be free.'

"'But Lord,' we say, 'we *like* mangoes. Why don't you give us your gift first? Then we promise we'll throw the mangoes away.'"

This is the essential conflict in every human heart. Part of us wants to reach out for the highest, but part cannot let go of our little personal desires. Consciousness is split in two – between our higher and our lower natures, between the selfless and the selfish. And the Lord tells us simply, "Make yourselves whole. Make me your only goal." Don't do anything just to please yourself; don't do anything just to please Tom, Dick, and Harry. Everything should be for the sake of the Lord, in you and in those around you.

In this – and here the mystics of all traditions speak with one voice – there is no room for doubts or reservations. I once read a remark that the Ten Commandments are rapidly becoming the Five Suggestions. This is the contemporary approach: we just don't like to be told what to do. So why not have Moses say, "Here are Five Suggestions for your careful consideration, for those who have the time"? Here the Lord says, "No exceptions. Give me everything: not only the big things, even the trifles. 'Thou shalt love the Lord with all thy heart and all thy spirit and all thy strength.'"

For the most part, this is not something we can do on the surface level of personality. We need to get into the very depths of consciousness, where the fierce desires for personal satisfaction arise. Meditation enables us to enter these levels, but meditation by itself is not enough. Once we break through the surface of consciousness, we come to places where we can neither go forward nor withdraw. We see the doors to deeper awareness there in front of us, but we don't know how to open them. We need both hands, and one hand is still hanging on to something personal, something private, that we don't want to leave behind. Until we let go, we are saying in effect, "Yes, Lord, I *would* like to go forward – just as long as I can stay here too."

No one has described this more vividly than Augustine. At the time of which he is writing, in his *Confessions,* Augustine is thirty-one. The storm within him has been going on for over twelve years. Now it is almost resolved, but he does not see that. All he can see is that the conflict has grown so fierce that he feels torn in two. "I was bound," he exclaims –

> not by another man's chains, but by my own iron self-will. My capacity to desire was in enemy hands, and he had made a chain of it to hold me down. For a will that is bent awry becomes selfish desire, desire yielded to becomes habit, and habit not resisted becomes compulsion. With these links joined one to the other . . . a hard, hard servitude had me in its grip. The new will being born in me . . . was not yet strong enough to overcome the old will that had been strengthened by so much use. Thus two wills warred against each other within me – one old, one new; one physical, the other spiritual – and in their conflict they wasted my spirit.

Then, with penetrating insight, he gives us the clue to victory:

> I was in both camps, but there was a little more of me on the side I approved than on the side I disapproved . . . for it had become more a matter of unwillingly experiencing [my desires] than of doing something that I actively wanted. . . . It was I who willed and I who was unwilling: it was I. I did not wholly will; I was not wholly unwilling. Therefore I strove with myself and was distracted by myself. . . .

The analysis is perfect. It is not two selves in conflict; it is one self – sometimes on one side, sometimes on the other. And to win, all we have to do is put more and more of ourselves in the other camp. Every time we withdraw our desires from some self-centered activity, a little more of us has defected from the side of darkness to join the side of light.

The dynamics is simple; but to do this, especially at the deeper levels of personality, is terribly, terribly hard. For a long time we cannot even see our choices clearly; we cannot bring our will to bear. In the latter stages of spiritual development, even the greatest mystics have cried out from the depths of their heart when they see how far off the goal is and how frail their strength, how limited their capacity. As Augustine says, it is like trying to wake up out of the seductive torpor of a dream – knowing it is time to wake up, longing to see, but unwilling to open our eyes. If we could watch our dreams, we would see that there is no freedom in the unconscious; our dream actions are all compulsive. And Augustine says, it is the same in waking life: our will is not our own.

> By this time I was certain that it would be better to give myself to your grace than to yield to my own desires. But though the former appealed to me and convinced me intellectually, the latter still ruled my wishes and bound me. I was still stuck for an answer to him who said, *Wake up, sleeper, and rise from the dead, and the Christ will give you light.*

In these verses the Lord is answering a practical, penetrating question: when we are immersed in this dream, how is it possible to wake up simply by willing it? We may see our choices clearly enough on the surface, but deep in the unconscious our will is fast asleep, and we want to go on dreaming. Here intellectual understanding is not enough. "We require," says St. John of the Cross, "a more ardent desire and a nobler love" – something that means more to us than the petty, passing satisfactions of the senses; something we desire so deeply that we are willing, in the end, to give up every self-centered attachment to obtain it. This is the supreme purpose of an incarnation of God: to draw us forward with such "burning fervor," as St. John says, that when the time comes to leave some personal desire behind us, we let go so eagerly that we do not even look back.

The French mystic Blaise Pascal brings this out beautifully in a little note he wrote towards the end of his life, after an experience of the unitive state. His language bears the unmistakable stamp of personal experience. For about two hours, it seems, his individual personality has been consumed in the intense fire of union with the Lord. Then the fire subsides; the experience comes to an end. But the proof of its reality is that now he is prepared to pay any price for making that experience permanent.

He puts it very movingly: *"Mon Dieu me quitterez vous?"* My Lord, are you leaving me? You come and fill my heart with joy and then you abandon me; what kind of cruelty is that? *"Que je n'en sois pas séparé éternellement?"* Shall we then be separated forever? I know now what it is like to be united with you, and I cannot bear to be separate again. How can I possess this joy forever? . . . And then he answers himself with words that are pure mysticism: *"Renonciation totalle et douce"*: renunciation, complete and sweet. When we finally want to be united with the Lord more than anything else, there is no longer any bitterness in giving up our attachments. It is sweet – not because there is no pain in it, but because it takes us closer to the object of our love. The Sufi poets put it beautifully: "When the heart grieves over what it has lost, the spirit rejoices over what it has found."

In the final stages of meditation we need such dedication, such total trust, to let go, that in my own small experience I have no doubt I would have found it impossible without the all-consuming love I developed for Sri Krishna. I was not born with this kind of love. I learned it, through the long, hard process of withdrawing all my personal desires from every selfish channel and redirecting them to flow towards my Lord. In every tradition, we have the testimony of men and women who have learned to do this and crossed the chasm of separateness into the unitive state. And Augustine's words can strengthen all of us when he exhorts himself, "Can you not do what these others have done? Or could they have done it by themselves, without the Lord their God? . . . Cast yourself upon him and do not be afraid; he will not draw away and let you fall."

This is not blind faith. It is tested continually as spiritual experience deepens, and those who have made their faith unshakable – great saints like Sri Ramakrishna, Francis of Assisi, Teresa of Avila – tell us pointedly from their own experience that their divine Beloved is much more real than we are. Physical reality is superficial: it is all a matter of physics and chemistry, a world of constant change. And the mystics say with one voice, "That alone is real which never changes." The body will perish, the universe itself is transient; but the Self in each of us will never pass away.

With infinite tenderness, the Lord is leading us in these verses to the theme of death and immortality. As long as we hold on to the passing pleasures of the physical world, we cannot avoid the suffering that overtakes the body in the course of time. In the first half of life, we have a certain margin for learning this – a certain amount of time to assess the value of physical satisfactions and weigh what they promise against what they actually give. But as we grow older, if we fail to assess wisely, life is not going to ask us if we are ready to give up our attachments. It is going to take them from us, and in that taking lies most of the suffering of old age and death.

Here, I think, my spiritual teacher – my grandmother – was at her best. I didn't think of her in those days as my spiritual teacher, of course. She was just my granny, who understood life better than anyone else I knew. And she knew just how to reach me. Even as a boy, when I would try to hang on to something she would ask, "Don't you have a sense of self-respect? Why do you have to be forced to make choices that you can make voluntarily? Don't let life back you into a corner and rob you. Give these things up now, when you are strong. That is the way to be free."

On the spiritual path we let go of all our selfish attachments little by little, according to our capacity – not under duress, but of our own free will – until finally we no longer need to hang on to anything else for support. To be forced to surrender is bitter. But to give up something for one we love, though at first it may seem a cup of sorrow, is found at last to be immortal wine.

"Wake up, sleeper, and rise from the dead, and the Christ will give you light." This is the promise of all the great religions: when we unify our consciousness completely, we pass beyond the reach of change and death into eternity. East and West, the language is the same. "Wake up!" says the Compassionate Buddha. "It is time to wake up. You are strong and young in heart; why do you waver?" The alarm is ringing, and no one can sleep forever; it doesn't behoove us to pull the blankets over our heads. And when we are awake at last, all we can do is rub our eyes. What once seemed day is now the night of ignorance. We have been living in our sleep. Now, as St. Teresa says, we live in "the light that knows no night," in a day that never ends.

PART TWO

The Still Mind

6 *Still your mind in me, still your-self in me, and without doubt you will be united with me, the Lord of Love, dwelling in your heart.*

IN MY CLASSES in India, I had two brothers who were excellent soccer players. They knew each other so well that they seemed to communicate at another level of consciousness; they played as one.

After a particularly good game, I went up to them and said, "Good show! Why don't you use that same concentration at school? That's all you need to get top marks."

They just laughed. "To tell the truth," one replied, "we don't know how we do these things. We don't even think about it. Our feet do everything; we just watch."

Ask any champion athlete. With some self-knowledge, she will tell you the same thing: "When I'm playing, my mind doesn't play a part." If the mind does step in, the consequences can be disastrous. You worry about losing; you remember something your boyfriend said or a remark some newscaster made about your game. Concentration goes, and you begin to make mistakes. If you try to reason while you're playing, you're lost. You can't afford to stand there deciding what to do: "Shall I pass or head it – or try to dribble? I guess I should pass, but who is clear?" By the time you have made up your mind, you will be in the middle of the next play.

All of us understand this when it comes to physical skills, but when the mystics talk about a still mind and living skills, we think they want us to become zombies. It is quite the opposite. Just as an athlete comes to life on the playing field when he or she can play without thinking, we come to our full stature as human beings only when the mind becomes still. The reason is simple: the only source of mental agitation is the ego. A still mind means a still ego – and when the ego is still we can see clearly, we are free from compulsions, and there are no barriers to interfere with our personal relationships.

Here it is helpful to look at the relationship between love and self-will – the shrill, overriding demand to put ourselves first, do as we like, think what we want, and get whatever we desire no matter what the cost might be to those around us. Clearly, the more self-will we have, the harder it is to love. So in order to love, we have to reduce self-will – and if we are not reducing self-will, no matter what else we are doing, we are not learning to love. All the verses in this chapter have one unifying theme: making the mind steady, especially in relationships, by rising above self-will.

The less self-willed we are, the more detached we become – not from others, but from ourselves. Without detachment from ourselves, we get easily caught up in our own reactions. Then it is easy to become jealous, or to lose interest in a person, or to become resentful when we don't get our way. On the other hand, the more detached we are from ourselves, the easier it is to remember the needs of others, without which love is impossible.

Most of the time we can think of the mind as a seesaw that is constantly in motion, swinging up when things go the way we like and down when they do not. Gradually, as self-will subsides and detachment rises, this seesaw motion becomes less and less erratic. At times we even find there are periods between upswings and downs when we can rest a little. Then we discover that these swings, both ups and downs, are disturbances in the mind's native state of balance, when it is still, calm, and full of quiet joy. When the mind is still, there is no self-will, no separateness, no sense of compulsion. We live in unity, and the natural expression of unity is love – not just love for one person or another, but love for all people, all life. This is our native state. It is not necessary to acquire anything to become loving: when all self-will is removed from the personality, what remains is love.

This is an inspiring picture, but more than that, it can be practiced – by all of us, even those whose minds are far from calm.

To begin with, the Lord says, "Still your mind in me." In practice, the meaning is simple: if you want to rest your mind in the Lord, don't try to rest it on the ego. In other words, don't brood on yourself.

This kind of brooding can come up in many ways. It may be self-righteous reflection on the past: "Why doesn't so-and-so behave the way I want?" It may be a fear of what somebody will say, or a bewitching memory, or a fantasy of MGM Studios calling on the phone, or a thousand and one other things. The content of these thoughts varies endlessly, but the focus is always the same: *I, I, I.* Whenever we dwell on ourselves like this, we are trying to rest our mind on the ego. The minute you catch yourself doing this, start repeating the mantram – the "prayer word" or Holy Name.

It takes time and practice to recognize these thoughts for what they are. As detachment increases, however, you discover that there are only a few basic themes with innumerable variations. One of the most popular themes with everybody is "I Don't Like It." Whether the "it" is breakfast cereal or the way your friend laughs, the emphasis is always on the "I." So as soon as you catch yourself thinking "I don't like this" – or especially "I don't like you" – don't stop to ask whether the opinion is legitimate or not; just repeat the mantram. Gradually, as you become more vigilant, the mantram will come to your rescue more quickly and more often.

I saw a good illustration of this when my wife and I were visiting our garden where our vegetables have attracted a number of gophers who are completely unintimidated by our presence. If they put their heads up and see me standing nearby, they don't hesitate; they come right up and go about eating whatever they like. But our cat is another matter. When they pop up their heads and see that Charles is around, he has only to give one little smile and the gophers disappear.

That is how the mantram should be. In the early days, a selfish thought will come up and nibble away at our attention until it is full. Then, after retiring for a nap, it comes back out of its hole again for more nibbling, all in its own sweet time. That is what agitation is: a thought burrowing in and out of consciousness as it likes, eating whatever it wants. But once we remember to bring the mantram on the scene, the thought will disappear. As we become more alert, the gap between the gopher popping up and Charles smiling – between the thought and the mantram – will narrow, until the response is immediate. That is a promising state, because it means that soon all our negative thoughts will go looking for quieter turf.

The intellect too – judgment, discrimination – has to learn to rest in the Lord. Otherwise there is still the possibility of turmoil. This doesn't mean that the intellect should be put to sleep. But to function well, it needs to refer its decisions to a frame of reference higher than the ego. The intellect's job is to make discriminating judgments: "What are the implications of this particular action? What will follow if I do this, or if I do not do that?" To function this way, it needs an overriding goal against which to compare and evaluate. Without a goal, it is liable to stay in its own little closet splitting hairs while the mind – our desires – makes all the decisions, mostly on the basis of "I like this" and "I don't like that." In practical terms, don't judge things only by your own interests; look at the needs of the whole.

People sometimes ask me, "How can we know what a higher perspective is? We don't even know where to look." This is a fair question: after all, most of us seldom look at life from any perspective other than our own. Here there are a number of questions you can ask. For one, whenever you are about to do something – or are already in the middle of doing something that you like very much or that is getting your mind all excited – ask yourself, "Whom will this really benefit?" You may get some rather partial testimony from the ego: it's all for the other person's benefit in the long run, simply a coincidence that it's what you really want too, and so on. But that is the purpose of the intellect, to be an impartial judge – to listen carefully, ask penetrating and embarrassing questions, and finally, when necessary, render a sternly worded judgment: "This doesn't benefit anybody, not even yourself."

This isn't to say that you shouldn't care about your own legitimate needs. But don't go exclusively after your personal benefit. Keep the needs of the whole in view; then your own needs are included automatically. When you can do this always, continuously, you won't even have to think about personal needs; they are taken for granted in the overall picture.

Second, take a long view of everything. The ego is shortsighted. It can't see past the end of its nose, because it is all caught up in what it can get for itself right now. But when you pull back a little from short-term promises, you get a little detachment from yourself. Then you can look far down the chain of cause and effect to see the long-term result of your actions – not only the result on the doer, but on others too.

Once we get past our early twenties, for example, I think most of us will have singed our fingers often enough to conclude that a flame is likely to burn. Especially where pleasure is concerned, it can be helpful to ask simply: "What does this promise and what has it actually delivered, to the best of my knowledge?" You can make a ledger and draw your own balance: "One German chocolate cake. Promise: gourmet ecstasy. Delivered: fifteen minutes of gooey sweetness, followed by stomach-ache, surrealistic dreams, and two pounds of extra weight." It can help, even with a powerful desire like sex. But it's not enough simply to analyze on the surface. You have to look deep within yourself and take a long view to see the total picture: what it promised and what it actually gave, not simply the next day but two years, ten years later.

Third, remember the injunction of the previous verse, where the Lord pleads, "Make me your only goal." Everything can be referred to that. "Will this deepen my meditation, improve my concentration, make my mind more even, make me less self-centered?" If so, I will do it; if not, I won't. "Will this divide my attention, isolate me from others, make me more speeded-up, activate an old memory or desire?" If so, I won't do it, no matter how pleasant or how innocent it may seem. Keep these words from the Katha Upanishad, one of India's scriptures, always in mind: "Pleasure is one thing; wisdom is another. The first leads to sorrow, though pleasant at the time. The latter, though at first unpleasant, leads to lasting joy."

More subtly, keep things in perspective. When you get caught in a particular activity or a particular person, you lose sight of the whole picture. One small part of life becomes blown up out of proportion, and all the rest shrinks into the background. It is difficult to keep the whole picture in view unless you have an overriding goal, but when you do, you can measure all your priorities against it.

To take one small example, look at running. Everyone in the Bay Area today seems to be not just jogging but training for a marathon. At the Bay to Breakers race in San Francisco, a distance of some seven and a half miles, literally thousands of people show up to take part. Now, I am all for physical fitness; who isn't? It is important for everyone, and it is especially important for those who are meditating seriously. But after all is said and done, running can be only a part of life. If this is forgotten, there is the danger of filling your life with running at the expense of other priorities. I would apply the same criterion to running as to every other human endeavor: "How much does this help me to realize the goal of life?" That is the measure of its value and the index of its priority.

One of the surest enemies of a long perspective is worry. On the San Francisco side of the Bay Bridge there used to be a big sign with a message from a great Indian mystic of this century, Meher Baba: "Do your best. Don't worry. Be happy." I suppose most of the people crossing that bridge in rush hour traffic thought Meher Baba was playing Pollyanna. He was not; he was being supremely practical. Worry is usually no more than self-will in one of its more subtle disguises. "Am I equal to this?" "Is so-and-so going to do that the way I want?" When you really are doing your best – in your meditation, in the other spiritual disciplines, at work, at home – there is no attention left over for worrying. Then you are beginning to rest yourself in the Lord at the core of your being.

All this can be effectively practiced in personal relationships. Wherever there is agitation in a relationship – vacillation, estrangement, doubt, reservation – the capacity to love is divided; love is not yet complete. "How much did you do for me today? How much did you put into the emotional till? Six cents? I'm going to count. If it is six cents, I'll give you six cents back. But if it's five, I'm not going to give you more than five." This is what we are accustomed to call love, even in some of the great romantic affairs of literature and history. But the mystics say, "That's not love; that's a commercial contract." It divides two people, and it divides consciousness. If you want to love, all these reservations have to go.

When your mind is still always – twenty-four hours a day, seven days a week, not only in waking life, but even in your dreams – then, says Sri Krishna, "You will live in Me continuously, absorbed in Me, beyond any shadow of a doubt." It is a state that is almost impossible to describe in words, but there are certain signs. For one, your awareness of the Lord will be unbroken. In a sense you will be meditating wherever you go, even if you are at your office or caught in the downtown shopping. Brother Lawrence's words are perfect:

> The time of business does not with me differ
> from the time of prayer, and in the noise and
> clatter of my kitchen, while several persons are
> at the same time calling for different things,
> I possess God in as great tranquility as if I were
> upon my knees at the blessed sacrament.

To put it another way, the well of your love will be always full and always flowing. It will be natural for you to love; it will be impossible for you not to love. You won't have to stop to think about how to respond to others. You will respond naturally, spontaneously, however is most appropriate for that person's long-term welfare. And in your personal relationships there will be no conflict, no doubts, no reservations, no irritation. You will not need to prompt or force your love, and you will need no reason for loving or trusting or forgiving. As St. Bernard says, love is its own reason. "Love seeks no cause beyond itself and no fruit; it is its own fruit, its own enjoyment. I love because I love; I love in order that I may love."

7 *But if you cannot still your mind
in me, learn to do so through the
practice of meditation.*

AT THIS POINT most of us would
like to explain, "I'd like to still my mind, but it
just keeps jumping around. Don't you know some
shortcut?"

The Lord says, "Of course. I'll give you a way
that has worked for spiritual aspirants all over the
world."

Expecting some great secret, we lean forward
eagerly. And the Lord whispers in our ear: "*Try* –
and keep on trying until you succeed."

This sounds hard – it *is* hard – but there is no
other way. Nothing about meditation is easy;
nothing takes place overnight. Even a giant like
the Buddha is said to have taken seven years to

attain nirvana – and if someone of his stature requires seven years, I think it is only reasonable for
people like you and me to be patient with ourselves
and admit that even a lifetime would not be too
long for this stupendous achievement.

Recently I read an advertisement for an "enlight-
enment workshop" that promised illumination in a
weekend. Being taken in by claims like these is
like thinking you can put on a pair of toe shoes
and make a guest appearance with the Bolshoi
Ballet without any practice or preparation. I once
saw a film of *Swan Lake* with breathtaking shots
of Rudolf Nureyev and Margot Fonteyn. When
Nureyev took one of his famous leaps, he seemed
to be suspended in midair. It looked so effortless
that I could almost imagine myself out there on the
stage, making wonderful leaps and breathtaking
glissades.

But another film – *The Children of Theater
Street,* about some of Russia's most promising
young ballet aspirants – opened my eyes. What
torture! Standing at the practice bar all day long,
kicking up your legs while the ballet master
stands there like a galley slave driver counting

"One, two, three! One, two, three!" It wasn't anybody's idea of effortless grace; it was just hard work.

That training, I understand, goes on for ten years or more. Often it starts at a very tender age. And once you make your professional debut, the work only becomes more arduous. Nureyev doesn't say, "I don't feel like it today." Whether he feels like it or not, he goes to the bar and practices – four, five, six hours every day. As I watched, I understood: this is the secret of excellence in anything. Spontaneity, effortless grace, comes only after years of practice. Dancers like Nureyev and Fonteyn are gifted, but the gift is not gracefulness; it is dedication.

Meditation is training the mind, which in many ways is like training the body. When you start jogging or doing sit-ups, at first you hear nothing from your muscles but complaints. It isn't because they are being overused, but because they have never been used. Similarly, when you try to concentrate in meditation, there are going to be taut tendons in your mind. If you have been impatient all your life and now start trying to be patient, your mind is going to ache all over. By the end of the day it will be begging you to stop. But I have never seen anybody who sincerely wanted better health say, "My tendons ache today, so I'm not going to run. I'm going to stay here in bed and give them a rest." Everybody knows that you just keep on running; soon the muscles become stronger and stop complaining. That is how it is with meditation. You keep working at it every day with the same enthusiasm and determination I saw in the faces of those students on Theater Street. There is no easy way.

I have to confess that I have developed a rather personal interpretation of this verse and the two that follow. The advice is explicit: "If you cannot still your mind, learn to meditate; if you can't meditate, serve me in those around you," and so on. But when it comes to something as important as Self-realization, I am the kind of person who won't leave any stone unturned. Even if it is only a little pebble, I have to turn it over. So even if the greatest mystics assure me that prayer or devotion is enough by itself, I will still say, "Excuse me. It may be enough for the Buddha or St. Francis, but a little person like me can't afford to take chances. I'm going to do everything I possibly can: meditate *and* put others first *and* learn to work without personal attachment, all together." I find this a very practical attitude, which I must have absorbed from my grandmother's example: there is always something more that you can do.

I remember well how I began to apply this. At first, I was like most beginning meditators: by the end of a hard day I would have used up most of the power released in my morning meditation. But for some time, it never occurred to me that I could meditate again in the evening. I had a full workload from morning to night. Even when the day was over, I would often return to campus after dinner to attend a faculty meeting or other college function. Naturally, when I did have a little time to myself in the evening, I liked to relax: read a favorite author, listen to classical music or the news, attend a play or lecture.

Once I realized I could do more to improve my meditation, however, my priorities underwent a change. When I saw that some of my distractions in morning meditation came from what was on my mind the night before, I set my Shakespeare aside, told All-India Radio it would have one less late-night listener, and started meditating regularly every evening too.

I didn't understand it at first, but I was beginning to make my day whole – which meant that I was making my consciousness whole as well. Now instead of just one slender thread connecting one morning's meditation with the next, my evening meditation picked up a fresh thread to the following morning. I could see the benefit almost immediately, not only in my morning meditation but in the quality of my life during the day.

To strengthen that new thread, instead of falling asleep in a Dickens novel, I started to read the great classics of world mysticism. I began with the *Gospel of Sri Ramakrishna,* an intimate record of the life of one of the greatest spiritual giants the world has seen. It wasn't easy to change my reading habits. I loved great literature passionately. But soon I discovered that although my love of literature was undiminished, I got much more from the words of a great saint like Sri Ramakrishna – simple, powerful, profound words that went straight to my heart.

It wasn't long before I was looking forward to my evening program: meditation and some spiritual reading, then falling asleep in the mantram. After that discovery, even if a favorite play came to campus I would tell my friends, "I'm sorry, I have another engagement."

That gave me the key: put meditation first. Make it your first priority; everything else can be second. Nothing important will ever suffer by this. "Seek first the kingdom of heaven and everything else will be added to it." Once I realized that, I began putting it into practice everywhere. I even used to meditate at noon when I could – right in the faculty room, seated quietly in a chair with my eyes closed, so that people must have thought I had been up all night reading Shakespeare and was catching forty winks. I wasn't; I was practicing the refrain of the Bhagavad Gita: "Make me your only goal." In ways like this I discovered that everybody has time for meditation, and every day is full of odds and ends of time that can be used for spiritual growth.

The key word here is practice. Try to keep your mind focused on whatever you are doing by bringing it back gently but firmly whenever it strays. This is not confined to meditation. It is essentially a matter of training attention. Trying to do this throughout the day throws light on every minute of daily living. It means we don't need to confine spiritual practice to a half hour or so in the morning and evening. We can train the mind wherever we are, whatever we are doing. The benefits are twofold: we unify consciousness by making the mind one-pointed, and by keeping it focused on what we choose, we keep from dwelling on ourselves.

In practical terms, this means gaining control over the thinking process itself. When we can finally put our attention wherever we choose, we can think whatever we choose. The implication is tremendous: we can become whatever we choose. As Ruysbroeck put it, we can be as spiritual as we desire to be – or as secure, or as loving.

Eventually – this is the ideal to be aimed at – the mind should not wander at all. Only then can it become still. When the mind wanders, consciousness is divided; attention is weaving all over the road.

Everybody knows what it is like to share the highway with a bad driver. He is driving along in the lane next to you and suddenly, without warning, he wanders into your lane. Perhaps his eye has been caught by a sign, perhaps he has remembered an errand; his mind may even be in a different county. Then, with equal abruptness, he realizes what he has done and overreacts – first with the brake, then with the accelerator – and darts back into his own lane.

If we could only see it, everything in life suffers like this when attention wanders. A mind that darts from subject to subject is out of control, and the person who responds to it weaves through life oblivious to others, running into difficult situations and colliding with other people. But the mind that is steady stays in its own lane. It cannot be swept away by an impulsive desire or fear, and because it stays completely in the present, it cannot be haunted by an unpleasant memory or by anxiety about the future. Most of our problems in life are caused by the mind weaving out of the here-and-now into a Never-Never Land of what was or might be or might perhaps have been. That is why I say there is no skill more worth learning than the art of directing attention as we choose.

In principle, it is simple to practice this. When the mind wanders, just bring it back to what it should be doing. The problem arises when the distraction is not some stray thought but compulsive: resentment, irritation, apprehension, craving. The power of such thoughts is that they are so self-centered. There is nothing the ego likes to do more than to think about itself, and when a self-centered thought comes up, everything in our conditioning screams, "Hey, look at this! Pay attention to this!"

Here again, our greatest ally is the mantram. Whenever a selfish thought comes up, repeat the mantram. When the mantram takes hold, the connection between the thought and your attention is broken. A compulsive thought, whether it is anger or depression or a powerful sense-craving, does not really have any power of its own. Thoughts, in this sense, are much the same. None of them has more muscle than the others. All the power lies in the attention we give. When we can withdraw our attention, the thought or desire will be helpless to compel us into action.

Attention is like a searchlight, mounted in such a way that it can be trained freely onto any subject. When we are caught up in ourselves – in other words, when attention becomes compulsive – this searchlight has become stuck. After many years of this, it is hard to believe that the light *can* turn. We think that compulsion is a permanent part of our personality. But gradually, all of us can learn to work our attention loose and train it where we choose.

One way to practice this during the day is to try to work cheerfully at jobs you dislike. This has nothing to do with the job; you are freeing your attention. Second, whatever you do, give it your best concentration – and, at the same time, learn to drop it freely when you need to shift your attention to something else. When you leave your office, for example, leave your work there too. Don't bring it home in a briefcase or, just as bad, in your mind.

Finally, the moment you take up something that does not require attention – doing the dishes, for example – start repeating the mantram. All this is the spiritual equivalent of those bar exercises in a ballet school. By practicing these skills, anybody can learn to direct attention freely. And when you can do this, you will never choose to focus it on yourself: not only because it brings such suffering, but because the ego, by its very nature, is such a crashing bore.

I like to illustrate all this by comparing the mind to a theater. Thoughts are the actors, and getting into the unconscious, if you like, is like going backstage into the greenroom, where everybody is getting made up. Anger is there putting on his long fangs, fear is rattling his chains, jealousy is admiring herself in the mirror and smearing on green mascara. And attention is the audience.

These actors are like actors everywhere: they thrive on a responsive audience. When jealousy comes out on stage and we sit forward on our seats, all eyes, she really puts on a show – if you want to see how much of a show, look at what happens in *Othello.* But what happens if nobody comes to see the performance? No actor likes to play to an empty house. If they're real professionals they might give their best for a couple of nights, but after that they're bound to get a little slack. Jealousy doesn't bother with her makeup any more; who's going to admire it? Anger throws away his fangs, fear puts away his chains; whom can they impress? Finally the whole cast gives it up as a bad job and goes out for a midnight cup of hot chocolate.

In other words, when you can direct attention, problems will never be compulsive again. I wish I could convey what freedom this brings. No matter how severe the problem, how painful the experience, how powerful the craving, you will be able to go to your meditation room and get up after meditation with all sense of oppression gone and your mind refreshed. That is the beginning of freedom in life. There may still be shackles on your hands, but now you know from your own experience that though it may take a long time and a lot of effort, every one of them can be removed through the systematic practice of meditation and the allied disciplines.

8 *If you lack the will for such
self-discipline, engage yourself
in selfless service of all around
you, for selfless service can lead
you at last to me.*

HERE AGAIN, my application of
this counsel is personal but practical. Even in the
early days, I have to confess that my capacity
for concentrating in meditation was rather good.
I had some excuse for convincing myself that
these words were not meant for me. Instead, I
took it personally. This helped my meditation
greatly, and that is why today I never talk only
about meditation; I always say "meditation *and*
its allied disciplines." Meditation is the foundation
of my eight-point program, but meditation is not
enough. The task of training the mind is so difficult that we need the support of a comprehensive

set of spiritual practices that work together all the twenty-four hours of the day.

Again, I can illustrate this from my own experience. When I began meditating morning and night, I could have been excused if I had decided not to try to squeeze any more into my day. But as I said, I don't like to leave any stone unturned. So when I saw an occasion when I could be of help to someone around me – by taking time to be with a student, for example, when he was in the hospital – I took a detached look at my schedule and told myself, "Well, you don't have to go to that movie on Saturday. You don't have to attend this concert on Friday night." I don't say that there wasn't a pang or two, especially when I had to miss an event I had been looking forward to. But the rewards more than made up for any momentary sense of loss. For one, my meditation deepened. Often I would notice the difference the next morning. But more than that, there was a fierce joy in turning my back on myself to help people. I know that in a sense I was not doing it for them personally; I was doing it for the Lord in them.

Gradually, I began to understand that serving the Lord in everyone around was not restricted to reading to the sick or feeding the poor. It meant, in the simple words my grandmother used, putting other people first. Once my eyes were opened, I didn't need special occasions to practice this. There were opportunities every day – on a busy day, many times every hour. Gradually I began to understand why this is so important for training the mind. When you are really focused on another person's needs, you forget yourself. Forget yourself completely, and you are united with the Lord.

The more I read in world mysticism, the more I appreciated the penetrating practicality of this approach. When all is said and done, I doubt very much if any of us in the modern world is able to extinguish the fierce fire of self-will without the benefit of personal relationships. In many traditions, the approach is what has been called the *via negativa:* trying to reduce the ego by a direct assault. This can work for a giant like St. Francis of Assisi or St. Thérèse of Lisieux, but most of us need some positive motivation that we can grasp – and even when we have the motivation, it is almost impossible to forget yourself when you live in a world of one. But where there is already a loving relationship, even between friend and friend, it is natural to want to put the other person first at least part of the time. I don't say it is easy. But it *is* natural and fulfilling, because the desire for unity is already there. Because the two of you have things in common, you can identify with him; you can find joy in contributing to her welfare. This is the *via affirmativa,* the positive way, which emphasizes not what is lost but what is gained.

There are some important things to remember when trying to put this into practice. To begin with, putting other people first does not mean saying yes to everything they say and do. I repeat this often because it has a vital place in love. In fact, saying yes to everything can be the opposite of love because it is not always in the other person's real interests. To love, we have to learn the art of saying no tenderly but resolutely when those we love are about to do something that can only bring them sorrow.

Most of us fall short of this, even in our most intimate relationships. Often, instead of saying no, we remark casually, "When you have time, will you turn this suggestion over in your mind?" Or we write a little note: "This passage from Corinthians may be of interest to you." This is called dropping a tactful hint, but unfortunately nobody notices these hints and nobody picks them up.

To me vague remarks like this show lack of love, because they are made out of fear of how the other person might respond. If someone we love is about to do something harmful to himself or others, we should have the security to say, "Even if you don't speak to me for a month I'm going to stand in your way, lovingly but firmly, until you change your mind." At the time this may be a source of irritation. But after that person has a chance to cool off, she will know she has a friend who really cares about her lasting welfare.

This doesn't apply only to domestic relationships. It can be practiced between friends, with co-workers, even between doctors and patients. I learned this in my early days as a teacher. Boys and girls used to arrive at college fresh with the simplicity of Indian village ways, and sometimes, after a little exposure to a wider world, they would get caught in activities that could only bring them sorrow in the long run. Some of my colleagues insisted that it was not my responsibility to intrude into my students' lives. "You're not their father," they said. "You're here to teach them Shakespeare and syntax." For a while I accepted this as the voice of experience. But I had a deep love for those students, and in turn they came to love me and trust me. It hurt me to see them hurt, and quite naturally, without doubt or vacillation, when I saw that they were about to get into trouble I would take them out for a walk, talk to them, and help them to see more clearly the consequences of what they were about to do. It wasn't always easy for them to accept this kind of loving criticism, but I don't think any of my relationships suffered. On the contrary, my students and their families came to appreciate me for it. "He's not just trying to please us," they would say. "He really cares what happens."

People sometimes ask me, "How can we tell how to put somebody else first?" I don't think there is any special secret to this. The same answer is given in all the world's great religions, but I particularly like the phrasing of the Compassionate Buddha: "Remember that what hurts you hurts others too. What irritates you irritates others too." People may differ in their preferences for salad dressing, but nobody likes a joke at his expense. No one likes to be talked about behind her back. No one likes to be ignored when he says hello, or to be talked down to, or to be interrupted in what she is saying or doing. Everybody is hurt by rudeness, irritated by an angry word, agitated by being rushed or pressured. One Western mystic sums it up in a simple phrase: "Be kind, be kind, be kind." That is the sum and substance of putting others first.

What keeps us from doing this? The Sanskrit language has a one-word answer: *samskaras*. A samskara is a compulsion, a rigid, automatic response to life which we think of as a permanent part of personality. But the samskara itself is not rigid; it is a process. A samskara is nothing more than a thought repeated over and over a thousand times, leading to words repeated a thousand times, resulting in action repeated a thousand times. A person with an anger samskara, for example, is prone to anger over anything. His behavior has very little to do with external events; by conditioning, anger has simply become the way his mind responds to life. By thinking angry thoughts, saying unkind things, and finally indulging in hostile behavior, he has made himself an angry person.

A kind of neurological shortcut has been dug in his mind, down which consciousness flows automatically to the same conditioned response.

What we call personality is nothing more than a collection of samskaras. In other words, we are what our samskaras are. It is a revealing but hopeful analysis. On the one hand, it means that there is very little freedom in what we do or even what we think. But on the other hand, it means that personality is not really rigid. Like the samskara, it too is a process. Though we think of ourselves as consistently the same, we are actually remaking ourselves every moment by what we think, just as the tissues of the body are in a constant state of repair and change. Usually, because of our samskaras, we go on remaking the same old shaky structure. But every thought is an opportunity for choice. Just as a samskara is built up through repeated thoughts and words and actions, it can be unbuilt through repeated thoughts and words and actions of the opposite kind.

In practice, this means that if someone provokes you and you respond with anger, you are actually making your anger samskara stronger. Even if you avoid that person afterwards, you are making the samskara stronger because it will be that much more disruptive in all your relationships in the future, and that much more difficult to overcome. So the mystic's attitude is truly radical: when you feel angry towards someone, that is all the more reason to be kind. It's not simply being kind to that particular person. You're being even kinder to yourself because you are undoing a compulsion, taking one more step towards being free.

Until we are free from our compulsions, we are like hand puppets; the samskaras are the puppeteers. We may think we choose to get angry – I have actually had somebody tell me this. But it would be more accurate to say that the anger samskara is doing everything: putting its fingers up into our arms and head (say, where the amygdala is) and making us throw crockery about, slam the door, and use words that are anything but kind. This is an apt illustration, because it is the nervous system itself that has been conditioned. But it can be deconditioned, and when it is, we are free.

The deconditioning process is straightforward enough: when a samskara comes up, don't act on it. When it tries to tell you what to do, say no. Repeat the mantram, go out for a long, brisk walk if possible, and throw yourself into hard, concentrated work, preferably for the benefit of someone other than yourself. When you can shift your attention to your work or to the mantram, you have shifted it away from the samskara. Immediately the samskara is weakened a little, and the will to resist is strengthened.

Conversely, if you do act on the samskara it is strengthened, and you have struck a blow at your own will. To put it another way, we cannot choose to stay out of the ring. The question is, who are we going to strike at, the samskara or ourselves? When we act on a samskara, we have landed a blow. The trouble is that we have injured the wrong party.

If you really want to land a blow at a samskara, go against it. Do just the opposite of what it says. This is a daring approach that appeals to me deeply. If somebody has been unkind to you, go out of your way to be kind to him. It can require a lot of endurance simply to be patient with such a person, but I'm talking about more than endurance now; I'm talking about daring. Try it. There is an exhilaration in it, and a special delight in seeing the other person rub his eyes in disbelief. "I was just rude to that chap, and now he's being thoughtful. Is he out of his mind?" Few people can go this far, but there is the same keynote in those marvelous words of Jesus: "If someone takes your coat, give him your cloak as well; if he makes you go a mile with him, go with him two."

Samskaras go deep into consciousness, and the will and intellect usually operate only on the surface. We may say in all sincerity, "I'll never get angry again!" But the samskara asks smugly, "Says who?" We don't even see these forces lurking in the unconscious, and if we do get a glimpse of them, we don't recognize them for what they are. It is only below the surface of consciousness in meditation that we begin to encounter samskaras without their makeup on. For a long time, vision is blurred in those depths. But when you get close to a samskara in meditation, there are certain external signs.

For one, there is a period of expectancy. You are about to get into trouble, about to repeat some conditioned pattern of behavior which you will later regret, and your subconscious is on the lookout for an opportunity. Second, concentration will be more difficult. Your attention will be scattered; it will be hard to keep your mind on a job, and you will find all sorts of excuses for putting off jobs that you don't want to do. And in meditation, it will be especially difficult to keep your mind on the passage. Attention will wander, and if you are not vigilant you may follow a distraction for a long time or even fall asleep.

Like road signs, all these signs have an explicit meaning: "Go Slow. Drive Carefully. Samskaras At Work." That is the time to be especially vigilant about all your spiritual disciplines. Be regular in meditation, use the mantram as much as possible, and work hard during the day, giving everything your one-pointed attention and enthusiasm. Be careful not to get speeded up or to allow your senses too much license. And especially, don't get caught in brooding on yourself. When you do that, you are inviting the samskara to come in and stay as long as it likes.

Undoing a samskara is the most challenging battle a human being can face. If you have been impatient for many years, for example, learning patience can be excruciating. At the end of the day, if you've really been trying hard, every cell in your nervous system will be crying out for rest. Samskaras can erupt anywhere, everywhere, and they don't pay attention to the rules of Queensberry. They'll hit you from behind, below the belt, in your sleep; they'll gang up on you; it's all open street fighting. The fight can be terribly dispiriting, especially when you get below the surface level and see how powerful these forces really are.

But there is a positive side too. This is the opportunity you have been waiting for. Every time you come face to face with a samskara, it is an opportunity to change yourself. The reversal in outlook is revolutionary. When you're tired, when people are provoking you, when your patience has worn thin and your morale is turning blue at the edges, you can rub your hands together with anticipation: you're in the ring at last, and the bell is about to go off.

Previously you might have said, "I don't want to go home now. The minute I walk through the door, I know I'm going to blow up. " Instead of going home, you'd be off to Redd's Recovery Room for a few rounds of bitter ale. But now you say, "Sure – one partner, two children, three people to try my patience. That's just the odds. Even if I miss one opportunity, I'm sure to have another."

The samskara may knock you around a few times, but as long as you keep on fighting like this, you're training. Your muscles are getting stronger, and the samskara, though it may not look any weaker at first, is taking the beating of its life. You are beginning to change your personality, and though the bigger samskaras are going to be in the ring for a good, long time, each round of the fight is bringing you closer to your goal.

9 *If you are unable to do even this,*
surrender yourself to me in love,
receiving success and failure with
equal calmness as granted by me.

THIS ADVICE sounds simple, but nothing is more difficult to practice. If it seems easy, that is because the idea of surrender has been so often misinterpreted. Surrender has nothing to do with doing nothing – and as for "just letting things flow," that is a state that is achieved only after years of almost superhuman effort. The spiritual life is a call to action: but it is a call to selfless action, that is, action without any selfish attachment to the results. In other words, it is not action or effort that we must surrender; it is self-will, getting our own way – and this is something that is terribly difficult to do. You must do your best constantly, yet never allow yourself to become involved in whether things work out the way you want.

It takes many years of practice to learn this skill, but once you have it, as Gandhi says, you will never lose your nerve. All sense of inadequacy goes – in fact, the question of "Am I equal to this job?" cannot even arise. It is enough that the job needs to be done and that you are doing your absolute best to do it. Then, no matter how stiff the challenges or how bleak the prospects, you can throw yourself into selfless action without conflict or diffidence or fatigue.

This is an elusive concept, and sometimes people ask me incredulously, "You mean you're not interested in the results of what you do?" Of course I am interested. I doubt that there is anybody more interested in his work than I am, because I know how much people can benefit from meditation. But after many years of practice, I have learned to do my best and then not worry about whether things will work out my way.

Worrying about results not only makes us less effective; it is futile. By our very nature we see only a small part of the total picture, and we make our plans on an appropriately narrow and egocentric scale. The result is usually about D minus, barely passing – unless, of course, somebody else is trying to get things his way too, in which case everybody runs the risk of getting an F. But when we learn simply to do our best and leave the question of success or failure to the Lord, the result can really be spectacular. Where we had something barely passing in mind, the Lord turns up with results that rate an A.

One of the most moving episodes in the *Ramayana,* one of India's great epics, illustrates this vividly. In just twenty-four hours, Prince Rama's life is turned upside down. He goes to sleep expecting on the following day to be crowned heir to his father's kingdom; the whole city is celebrating. But he wakes up to find that his stepmother has turned against him, and instead of receiving his birthright, he is sent into exile in a forest for fourteen years. Rama's brother is furious. But Rama pacifies him with a simple question. "Haven't you ever planned something down to the last detail – done everything you could to make sure nothing goes wrong – and then had the whole affair turn out completely differently? Doesn't that show you that there is a power in the universe that encompasses us all, that it is not possible to ordain our lives the way we will?"

If we could only stand back from our lives and take a much longer view, even the smallest events would be seen to fit into a vast picture in which, as Jesus says, every hair of our heads is numbered. There is no contradiction between this idea and free will. We are shaping our lives continuously by what we think and say and do. To his brother, Rama's banishment seems a disaster. But it is all part of a much larger drama. Many years earlier, by accident, Rama's father killed the son of an old sage. When Rama is banished, he loses his own son – and that same exile, which seems so cruel, proves to be the door through which Rama enters into his own glorious destiny. Shakespeare's words go deeper than he may have known: "There's a divinity that shapes our ends, rough-hew them how we will."

If I may say so, the Lord is a thorough teacher. When necessary, he will see to it that those who love him are tested from every quarter – as my grandmother used to say, not any more than they can bear, but never any less. For most of us, there is no other way to learn to remove selfish attachment from our life. When we are taking refuge under one corner and it caves in, we can always hide under another. If all four corners fall in, we can at least stand in the center. But when we are standing in the center, about to breathe a sigh of relief, and the roof falls in, we have nowhere left to look for help but inwards. And the amazing thing is that when we trust in this completely – *and* do our best – help always comes. It may not be in the way we expect it, it will not be at the time we expect it, but it will come; of that there is no doubt.

In a small way, this is the history of our own meditation center too. There were times in the early days when we faced nothing but obstacles – not only relevant obstacles, the kind one expects at the outset of spiritual work, but sometimes unnecessary, even silly difficulties too, which I think the Lord must have put in our path for no other reason than a Puckish sense of humor. At such times, I kept on reminding myself that it was not my work. From the assurances of all the world's mystics, I knew that all I had to do was empty myself of all self-will and put myself in the hands of the Lord; how he used my life after that was not for me to worry over.

Today, after many years of practicing this, I do not get upset over anything where the work of our meditation center is concerned. I have no doubt now that work that is free from all self-seeking has to prosper in the long run, though it calls for resourcefulness, discrimination, and a lot of dedicated effort.

This is not blind faith. It comes through many years of trial. When I first took to meditation, though I had the examples of my grandmother and Mahatma Gandhi to guide me, I had no experience of these truths myself. As my meditation deepened, I had to face some difficult decisions about the conduct of my life. At such times, I usually made the best choice I knew how, even when it was not particularly pleasant – and, like most ordinary people, I sometimes made wrong decisions that carried painful consequences.

After a while, however, I began to notice that if I had done my best to choose what was right, even when I made a wrong decision the consequences would be mitigated. Either I would surmount the difficulty through some turn of events, or the difficulty would prove to be an opportunity. It was not at all clear at the time, but now I can look back and see that all these difficulties were training me to do my best and leave the rest to the Lord. When you do this, you can be sure that things will work out for the best of all concerned. "After all," the Lord would ask, "don't you trust me? I who am responsible for the rhythms of the galaxies, if you are really trying to serve me, don't you think you can rely on me to give you whatever you need for spiritual growth?"

10 *Better indeed is knowledge than mechanical practice. Better than knowledge is meditation. But better still is surrender in love, because there follows immediate peace.*

THIS BEAUTIFUL VERSE wraps up the four which precede it. On the intellectual level, it may seem obscure. But after some years of practicing these disciplines, the meaning becomes clear if we remember that here, words like "knowledge" and "surrender" are not watertight categories. After all, where there is knowledge of the unity of life, there is love. Where there is love, there is a direct apprehension of unity. And unless the mind is stilled through meditation, it is not accurate to talk about either transcendental knowledge or love. All these are categories of the intellect, which cannot help dividing. But in practice they flow together, which is why I have no hesitation about recommending the approach I have found effective in my own life: to practice all of them together.

"Better indeed is knowledge than mechanical practice." This is not to deprecate mechanical practice: after all, at the beginning, the practice of any spiritual discipline is bound to be mechanical. If somebody comes to me and asks, "You want me to repeat the mantram *mechanically*?" I say simply, "Of course." How else can we repeat it at the start? In order to repeat the mantram with devotion, we must have very little self-will. But devotion can grow. We begin repeating the mantram with as much enthusiasm as we can, whenever we can, and after a lot of practice, it slowly begins to penetrate to a deeper level of consciousness.

Similarly with meditation. At the beginning, though it should never be mechanical, meditation is only on the surface. It takes a lot of regular, enthusiastic work to break through the surface and open up a channel into our deeper consciousness.

As we practice these disciplines, insight grows. We begin to see that living for ourselves has inescapable consequences for which we hadn't bargained: alienation, loneliness, deteriorating relationships, a sense of desolation. The more we grab for our own happiness, the faster it recedes. At the same time, we discover that when we go after the happiness of others, relationships improve, depression disappears, and we find it easier to face the challenges of life with resourcefulness and peace of mind. These discoveries are the beginning of wisdom – the deep insight into life that the Buddha calls *prajna*. We are beginning to see beneath the surface of life, through the bewitching illusion of separateness that keeps us isolated from the rest of life, and everything benefits: meditation, relationships, security, love.

But understanding is not enough. These insights need to be practiced. And for translating insight into daily living, we need meditation – not meditation on the surface now, but one-pointed concentration that drives spiritual ideals deep into consciousness and releases the power to act selflessly during the day.

As we practice this, the barrier of separateness is lowered and love grows. We ask less and less what we can get from life and more and more what we can give. After many years, if our practice of these disciplines has been sincere and systematic, we may reach a stage when we can truly say, "I love." All barriers are gone; every trace of self-seeking has been removed. We no longer seek anything for ourselves because we find our joy in the joy of all. Then, and only then, the heart is flooded with utter peace, "the peace that passeth understanding." The ego has been stilled, so there can be no more turmoil in the mind, no more vacillation, no more anxiety or fear.

This is not a temporary experience. Every corner of the personality is bathed in peace that cannot be taken away. Jesus says, "Peace I leave with you; my peace I give unto you: not as the world giveth, give I unto you." As St. Catherine of Genoa explains beautifully, out of the fullness of her own experience:

> When the soul is naughted and transformed, then of herself she neither works nor speaks nor wills, nor feels nor hears nor understands; neither has she of herself the feeling of outward or inward, where she may move. And in all things it is God who rules and guides her, without the mediation of any creature. And the state of this soul is then a feeling of such utter peace and tranquility that it seems to her that her heart, and her bodily being,

and all both within and without, is immersed in
an ocean of utmost peace. . . . And she is so full of
peace that though she press her flesh, her nerves,
her bones, no other thing comes forth from them
than peace.

PART THREE

The Faces of Love

11 *The one I love is incapable of ill*
will and returns love for hatred.
Living beyond the reach of "I and
mine," and of pleasure and pain,
full of mercy, contented, self-
controlled, firm in faith, with
all their heart and all their mind
given to me — with such as these
I am in love.

NOW WE ARE entering one of the most beautiful, precise, and practical descriptions of the man or woman of God that I have seen. The purpose of such descriptions is not merely to inspire us, but to show us our real potential as human beings: what kind of person you and I can actually become, in a marvelous transformation, through the practice of meditation and the allied disciplines.

In a sense, the words of an inspirational passage like this are not just words. They are more like depth charges that are set to go off when they reach a certain level of consciousness. In meditation, by the concentration we give, we drive each word deep into consciousness so that it can release its potential. But when these words explode, instead of causing damage, they heal. Internal conflicts are resolved, doubts and reservations fall away, and we get the certitude that we are equal to challenges from which we used to run away.

This does not happen overnight, and like most people who are meditating sincerely, I used to wonder at times if this explosion was ever going to take place in my own consciousness. After all, I reasoned, the words of the Gita are thousands of years old; even the best of ammunition can fizzle after the passage of time. But I went on giving my best every day, and eventually I reached a stage in meditation where I could almost feel these words trembling deep in my consciousness, ready to go off. I didn't know what was happening, but for a long time there was a strange air of expectancy. Then, one by one, each word released its potential, and I realized that the passage had become an integral part of my consciousness.

When translated literally, many of the words in these two verses sound negative: "without ill will for any creature, without any sense of 'I' or 'mine.'" But in this case, a negative construction in grammar has a wholly positive meaning in life. By not acting selfishly, speaking harshly, thinking negatively, we finally arrive at our native state, which is love itself.

In other words, this transformation does not take place by meditation alone. Meditation gives the power, but we then have to draw on this power to check every self-willed impulse during the day. Unless there are changes in our day-to-day behavior, even if they are modest and slow, we cannot talk about the transformation of personality.

You can see that this puts personal relationships in a wholly different light. From the spiritual perspective, if we are resentful towards a particular person, it is a much more serious problem than just one impaired relationship. That resentment is preventing us from attaining our native state. These verses do lead to deeper relationships, but their real purpose is much more: to enable us, through personal relationships, to realize the unity of life. If only in terms of our own spiritual progress, we need to learn to relate with kindness and consideration not only to a little clique of people whom we happen to like but to everybody: at home, at work, in the store, on the bus, wherever we are.

It is easy to write this, or to read it and nod approval. But to practice it, day in and day out, is a constant battle. The other day an acquaintance was telling me he had been a soldier for twenty-five years. I wanted to reply, "Me, too." The person who tries to live in accord with verses like these has been drafted into the toughest battle that life has to offer, and sent to the front lines without even a drop of rum.

Sometimes, riding my bicycle home from the university after a day of cross fire between department difficulties and student problems and all the university red tape, I used to think with a sigh of the spiritual aspirants in their caves on the Himalayas, watching the deer come to drink at a nearby brook and listening to the wind in the trees. I wouldn't really have traded places with them, because it is only the rarest of individuals in any age who can extinguish self-will in the solitude of a cave. But there is nothing easy about realizing the Lord in the midst of society either. From first to last, it is a battle – and in a sense, every word in these verses is a battle strategy.

The very first phrase gives the key to all the others: "incapable of ill will towards any creature." Just two words in Sanskrit, but look at the daring! It is not enough not to express ill will; we must become incapable of it. Who even considers this possible today? Ill will is probably the most insidious enemy anyone could face. It doesn't conquer us overnight, so that we wake up the next day with a different personality. It infiltrates consciousness with a few well-trained paratroopers: dislikes, resentments, petty, personal grudges. Paratroopers, as you know, wear camouflage, and the moment they land, they pretend they are part of the shrubbery. That is exactly what resentment does. It has all kinds of disguises, such as rationalization and righteous indignation. And like a good commando, it doesn't stay hiding in the bushes; it immediately tries to occupy the strategic centers of the mind. Judgment is one of the first to fall, and once judgment has been occupied by resentment, we do not see things as they are. We feel threatened where there is no danger, and where there is danger we don't see anything at all. After some time of this, the final occupation is easy. We welcome the enemy forces as liberators, and our loyal friends – equanimity, unselfishness, good will, trust – we treat with suspicion as traitors.

Even at this stage, I would say, it is possible to resist and win. But any strategist from Hannibal to Ho Chi Minh will say that if you intend to drive an enemy out, the least you can do is not first invite him in. In other words, don't wait until the mind is teeming with invading resentments. As soon as you see a hostile thought, shoot it down with the mantram. It doesn't matter if the thought seems justified or not; that is part of the camouflage. Don't stop to ask questions; don't wait for it to land and give you a password – shoot. At the beginning there may be a number of wild shots, but keep repeating the mantram until the thought drops out of sight. After a while, with a lot of practice, you will be able to pick off an invading resentment with just one shot.

At the heart of problems like this is our compulsive attachment to two narrow concepts: I and mine. This is the ego's vocabulary. It goes around with a little mental stamp like those you pick up in a stationer's, stamping everything and everybody it fancies: *Mine, Mine, Mine.* What it really means is *Me, Me, Me.*

Look at how people identify with their cars, or their clothes, or even their hairstyles. I have a close friend, for example, who is devoted to her old Volkswagen "bug." If I compliment her on it, she is pleased; if I tell her what Ralph Nader said about classic VWs, she feels insulted. Where is the connection? *She* is not a bug.

Or take the way some people feel about their hair. If you make a remark about my hair – or lack of it – my hair might have reason to bristle, but why should I? I am not my hair; and if I start identifying with my hair, or with anything else external, my ego would swell to such a size that it couldn't help bumping into other egos and taking offense.

This can be extended even to opinions, which is where many difficulties in personal relationships arise. Most of us identify ourselves with our opinions. Then, when we are contradicted, we take it personally and get upset. If we could look at ourselves with some detachment, we would see how absurd this is. There is scarcely any more connection between me and my opinions than there is between me and my car, and once we realize this at a deeper level of consciousness, most of the resentment caused by differences of opinion disappears.

This kind of detachment does not come easily, but it can be cultivated. Again, it may be helpful if I illustrate from my own life. In my earlier days – to change a few names – if Henry Ford, say, objected to my opinions on history and told me point-blank, "History is bunk," I used to get upset. After a few instances of this I would begin to think of Henry Ford not as the man who made Detroit, but as the man with irritating views on history. In other words, I would begin to make a simple, common, but disastrous equation: "Henry Ford *is* the opinion that history is bunk." Once this equation is drawn, it follows that if you dislike the idea, you have to dislike Henry Ford: and that is exactly what I used to do, except, of course, that I am using Mr. Ford here only as an illustration. After a while I would even block out his name; I would think, "Oh, you know, what's-his-name: the man who thinks history is bunk."

Now, I am not denying that there are people who are disagreeable about their opinions. Such people can be found in every walk of life, and it is only normal to avoid them. But the Gita is not talking about being normal; it is talking about living in freedom. And when I began to understand this, I said to myself, "Why not try sitting back from your opinions with a little detachment? After all, it doesn't mean you have to give up your opinions. You don't have to agree that history is bunk in order to move closer to Henry Ford." The real issue is not opinions at all; it is how to lower the barrier of self-will that keeps us from relating freely to everyone.

My desire to learn this was so great that if no one was around to contradict me, I used to seek out somebody whose ideas made my hair stand on end and say, "Hello, Henry, why don't you explain to me your views on history?" And instead of arguing, I would sit and listen carefully and draw him out with the utmost courtesy. It had several surprising consequences. For one, I discovered I didn't really mind the man after all. In fact, once I got my prejudices out of the way, I began to like him, simply as a human being. Second – which I hadn't expected – I began to understand his point of view. I didn't always agree with it, but I began to understand it; and that enabled me to listen with real interest, because it helped me to understand my own position better too. And third, even more unexpected, he began to listen with respect to me.

In other words, there is nothing wrong with disagreement. In fact, where relationships are concerned, it is a necessary part of love to disagree when the other person is about to do something he or she will later regret. What upsets us in such situations is simply lack of detachment: we don't know how to disagree with complete respect.

Though I have been in this country for many years now, there are still many American expressions I don't understand. I remember trying to explain meditation to a young fellow in Berkeley who kept shaking his head and saying, "Man, I just don't hear you." In all innocence, I started over again a little louder. Finally it dawned on me what he really meant: "I just don't *want* to hear you. I don't like what you're saying, so I'm going to plug my ears until you're finished."

This is what most of us do when there is disagreement. We carry around a pair of earplugs, and the minute somebody starts saying something we don't like, we stuff them in our ears until he or she is through. Watch with some detachment the next time you find yourself quarreling with someone you love. It won't look like a melodrama. A detached reviewer would write, "First-rate comedy! Two people trying to reach an understanding by not listening to each other." One is saying, "What did you do the other day when I said such-and-such?" And the other replies, "What about you?" Can you imagine anything more comical? They are not trying to settle their differences; they are trying to make sure they will never forget them.

If we could ask the mind on such occasions why it doesn't listen, it would answer candidly, "Why should I? I already know I'm right." We may not put it into words, but the other person gets the message: "You're not worth listening to." It is this lack of respect that offends people in an argument, much more than any difference of opinion.

But respect can be learned – again, by acting as if we had respect. And one of the most effective ways to do this is simply to listen with complete attention, even if we don't care for what the other person is saying. Try it and see: the action is very much like that of a classical drama. For a while there is the "rising action," just as I used to draw it for my students on the blackboard. The other person's temper keeps going up, language becomes more and more vivid; everything seems heading for a climax. But then comes the denouement. The other person begins to quiet down: his voice becomes gentler, his language kinder, all because you have not retaliated or lost your respect for him.

When detachment has deepened considerably, you can actually see the mental states behind a person's behavior. It is an extraordinary leap in human perception. Just as a physician makes a diagnosis from X-rays of a patient's lungs, you gain the capacity to read a kind of X-ray of a person's mind and understand why he or she is behaving in a particular way. When this comes with detachment, you stop judging others. Then you can begin uprooting ill will not only from your words and behavior, but from your very thoughts.

Fortunately, this capacity does not ordinarily come without considerable detachment from oneself. The reason is simple: without detachment, there is too much of the ego in the way for vision to be clear. This is a precious safety clause, because sometimes even behind pleasant words, the mental state is anything but pleasant. But when you look at a person's behavior with detachment, it's almost like seeing the inner mechanisms of a clock. Most of us, when we have a problem with a clock, don't throw it out the window. We turn it around and try to find out what has gone wrong. Here it is much the same. You still see the face of the clock – the dial, the hands, the pendulum swinging back and forth, the little bird sticking out its beak at you and saying "Cuckoo!" But now, instead of taking all this personally and getting angry, you can look behind the face to the mechanisms inside and see what has gone wrong. It releases great compassion, for as Voltaire says, "To understand all is to forgive all."

Some of the most beautiful words in the Sanskrit language are used here. *Karuna,* a favorite concept of the Buddha's, means the continuous flow of love and sympathy that comes when you see yourself in all and all in you. *Kshama* is mercy, a readiness to forgive everyone no matter who he is or what she may have done. This is much more than simply shaking hands and saying, "I forgive you." Real forgiveness flows automatically, and with it comes the desire and the capacity to move closer to those who offend you, and to help. And *maitra,* another of the Buddha's favorites, is real friendship, where you never withdraw your respect, never retaliate, but always see the best in others and help them to live up to the highest of which they are capable. This is what loving the Lord means in practice. When we try to live like this, we not only benefit those around us, we are helping to unite ourselves with the Lord once and for all.

12 *Not agitating the world or by it agitated, they stand above the sway of elation, competition, and fear, accepting life, good and bad, as it comes.*

"WHEREVER you go," my Granny used to tell me, "you are going to encounter ups and downs – pleasure and pain, fortune and misfortune, people who like you and people who don't care for you at all." The nature of life is up today and down tomorrow, and the Gita says simply, let it go up and down; you don't have to go up and down with it.

I see a lot of popular interest in biorhythms, the built-in cycles of emotional ups and downs that each of us is supposed to have. For two weeks I can be cheerful, but then for the next two weeks I have to go into a slump. If I'm irritable in those two weeks, I'm sorry, but I have to be irritable; that's just the way my cycles go.

The idea, of course, is that if you can plot these cycles, you can pursue your goals when you're at your best and stay at home in bed when you are not. Unfortunately, the demands of life pay very little attention to anybody's cycles. If they did, I doubt that we would ever learn to grow up, which in the Gita means being at our best always – loving when life is for us, equally loving when life is against us. This is just the opposite of a colorless existence. It means going beyond the conditioned cycles of excitement and depression to live in an abiding sense of joy.

Most of us do not think of excitement as a problem. After all, doesn't everybody like to be on cloud number nine? I agree: if we could stay on cloud number nine, life might be very pleasant. But as all of us know, the cloud eventually evaporates. Then we not only come abruptly back to earth; we usually burrow right into its depths and hide – that is, we go into a depression.

In other words, the problem with excitement is depression. "What goes up must come down" is as true of moods as it is of Newton's apple.

Excitement and depression are inseparable aspects of the same phenomenon, the erratic swinging of the mind: up with what it likes, down with what it doesn't like. Because of our conditioning, we like to make a distinction and say that when the mind swings up, the swinging is pleasant; when the mind swings down, it's unpleasant. But a spiritual scientist like the Buddha would say, "No. Swinging is swinging." In both excitement and depression the mind is in agitated motion, and if we let it get agitated over what it likes, it will stay agitated when it encounters – as it must – something it does not like. The agitation is the same; the focus of attention has simply changed.

This is an important point, because depression is almost epidemic today – a serious and widespread problem that often goes unrecognized when help is needed. From one fourth to one third of all persons experience some form of excessive mood disturbance at some time or other in the course of a lifetime; in perhaps as many as one person in ten, the disorder will warrant medical attention. And who can estimate the incidence of subclinical common "blues"?

In an important sense, however, I think most

kinds of depression are not really medical problems. There are drug approaches that can be effective first aid, but they do not get at the mechanisms of depression; they only affect its symptoms. Long ago, when Dr. Paul Dudley White, the distinguished American heart specialist, was asked what he considered the best treatment for heart disease, he answered simply, "Prevention." That is the best treatment for depression too, and for most of us it is entirely within reach.

There are a number of ways to illustrate how excitement and depression work. One way that throws light on the subject is to consider the role of the senses. We can think of the senses as windows. In my old state of Kerala, houses are mostly one-story buildings with large wooden windows, which open out onto verandas when weather is pleasant and which close securely during heavy rains or the oppressive heat of the afternoon. Windows made from good wood can function well for centuries, but those made from cheap wood pose a constant problem: after a little exposure to tropical heat and monsoon storms, they warp. Then they open only with difficulty, and there is always the danger of forcing them open so wide that they get stuck and can't be closed again. When that happens, you are at the mercy of all kinds of weather – until finally a good strong storm comes along and slams the windows stuck with a vengeance. After that, you can't easily get them open again. One minute you're wide open to the world, everything outside is blown right in; the next minute you're sealed inside.

The senses behave in a very similar way. They are windows into the mind, meant to open smoothly when we are interacting with the outside world and to close securely when they are not in use. But in a person who gets easily excited, the windows of the senses are not just opened gently. They are thrown open as far as they can go, because of the intense desire to take in all the stimulation of the outside world.

We are not usually aware of this when it happens, because all our attention is turned outwards; there is no attention left for reflection and self-knowledge. But what can happen is that the senses are thrown open with such force that they get stuck that way, leaving us completely at the mercy of the weather. We take in everything without discrimination; and just as we tried to take in what we thought was pleasant, we have to take in what is unpleasant too.

Then, eventually, there comes a storm. Something unpleasant comes along and slams the senses closed with a bang, locking us inside. That is depression.

What follows then is tragic: we cannot help brooding on ourselves. Mechanically, the senses continue to receive impressions – sights, sounds, and so on – but attention has turned completely inwards. If you look at a depressed person's eyes, you will see a little sign: "Closed. Nobody Home." There *is* somebody home, but he or she isn't answering any calls. You can take him to a movie and he won't respond; you can talk to her and she may not even hear: their attention is all caught inside, in brooding on themselves. There is even a characteristic expression, like the look on the face of somebody listening to music with a set of earphones, slumped down in a chair absorbed in a world of his own. Depression has its own kind of earphones. The ears are closed to the outside world and the person is hearing nothing, listening to nothing, except his or her own thoughts. The tragedy is that the program is never positive. Everything is in negative mode: "Nobody likes me, I don't like anybody, I can't stand myself."

In personal relationships, the tragedy is at its worst. In a sense, while we are in a depression, we are not aware of any relationship with those around us – which means, among other things, that we are cut off from the major source of joy and meaning in life. To relate to people, attention has to flow outwards to them, so that we can identify with them and include them in our world. But if the windows of the senses are closed, there is no connection with others at all. We can be in the midst of a jolly crowd and still feel utterly alone.

There is an interesting comparison here with meditation. There too the senses are closed down, and the mind is trained upon itself. But in meditation, this is done freely. You choose a time and place for going inwards, and coax the eyes and ears and other senses to sit still while your higher mind takes a close look at your lower mind and concludes with compassion, "What a clown!" All this is done in freedom, and after meditation you can turn your attention outwards again with the same freedom. But in depression, when the senses are slammed shut without your consent and the mind is turned in on itself compulsively, what happens is not a matter for joking. Everything is distorted, the way it is in a house of mirrors. Your partner looks as big as an elephant, you look like a little mouse; one side of you seems twisted and deformed. Smiles look like grimaces, and every gesture is threatening. If the bout of depression is prolonged, or if such bouts come frequently, you can even come to think that is how you and those around you really are.

Here, as usual, the approach of the Gita is very practical. Don't expect such people to be able to love, to be steadfast or patient or to work consistently at their jobs; show them how to get the windows open. Once that has been accomplished, you can teach them how to open and close their senses gently and with discrimination, so that they can guard themselves against depression coming again.

Essentially, the biochemical approach to depression is to force the windows open again, very much in the way in which they were slammed shut – that is, involuntarily. This approach can save lives, but it cannot do much by itself to change the habit of oscillation in the mind. This is the real problem, and unless this habit is changed, depression is bound to recur. But to change the habit, we have to learn to open and close the windows of the senses for ourselves.

There are innumerable ways to work on this, but here let me suggest just a few that are most effective in first aid. For one, don't isolate yourself; be with people. When you are in a depression, all your conditioning is crying out for you to lock yourself in your room, put on your headphones, and brood over how depressed you are. This may be natural, but it is probably the worst thing you could do. To open the sense-windows you need to come out, be with people, and give them your full attention. It is especially helpful if you can throw yourself into hard, selfless work with other people. Activity, especially hard physical activity, helps to keep your mind off yourself. And don't act depressed; act normal. Your mind may complain about the company – "a lot of crashing bores" – but you can still pretend to be interested. You don't have to talk, but you can at least listen with interest – and smile, even if you have to pull the corners of your mouth up with your fingers. You know you're really depressed, other people may know it too, but what does it matter? By acting normal you are becoming normal, freeing your attention from where it has been compulsively caught. The moment will come when you forget that you are acting. Then you are not acting any longer; the depression has lost its hold on you.

In all these approaches, the key is the same. A depressed person has lost the capacity to direct his attention. To get out of a depression, it is necessary to go against your conditioning and turn attention outwards again. When you can keep attention focused outwards, depression is gone; the windows are open again.

But there is another way to look on the mechanics of depression, and that is in terms of vital capacity. This is an extremely useful approach because it connects directly with the cause of depression: excitement.

The Sanskrit word I am translating here as "vital capacity" is *prana*, and I know of no real equivalent in English. For purposes of this discussion, prana can be compared with gas in a car. It is the energy of life, not only on the physical level but on the emotional level as well. And in terms of energy, being excited consumes a lot of gas.

This shows in many ways. There are people who,

as soon as they get excited about something, begin to talk and talk. Excitement means the mind is getting out of control, and the lack of control overflows into their speech. Other people simply get speeded up, trying to fit more and more into their day, their sentences, even their thoughts.

All this burns a lot of fuel, not only on the physical level but on the emotional level as well. If you could monitor your body when you're excited, you would see all sorts of signs that energy is being burned excessively. The heart beats faster, muscles become tense, breathing is rapid and irregular. It is like punching holes in your gas tank: in all these ways, vitality is draining out. That is why excitable people often feel harassed and tired as the day wears on, always busy but accomplishing comparatively little.

But as prana is drained, the capacity for excitement drops too. We may still be in the same surroundings – on the same cruise, with the same people, visiting the same Caribbean island – but what seemed exciting earlier now seems dull or irritating. This is depression. We have opened the valve on our prana tank, and after a while we find that there is no more fuel with which to generate attention. In general, unless we can reverse the conditioning of depression, it takes as long for the tank to fill up again as it took to drain it through our excitement.

To me, this is a precious safety mechanism. The conditioning of excitement is so powerful that without some kind of cutoff, most of us would go on getting excited and drain a lifetime of prana before it occurred to us that we were throwing away our capacity to live. In this sense it is possible to think of a mild depression as a friend, very much like indigestion. Without indigestion, many of us would overeat until it was difficult to reverse the damage. Similarly, a mild depression is a friend that is sending us an urgent reminder, special delivery: "You haven't been using your senses very well; you haven't been taking care of your mind. No more prana until you give your mind and body a rest." It isn't pleasant, but this gives a kind of recuperative period in which the senses close down so that our tank can fill up again.

One of the clearest illustrations of this is that depression often is marked by a drop in sexual desire. There is a direct connection, because no stimulus to excitement is more powerful than sex – not simply sex on the physical level but especially in the mind, where the desire arises. Dwelling on sex, anticipating it, longing for it, all takes up a lot of prana. When the tank is depleted for a while in depression, we get a breathing spell in which to consolidate vitality again and to learn to protect ourselves against undue excitement in the future.

But let me be clear on this point: it is not sexual desire that is the problem. It is excitement, the mind going out of control. Prana is drained by any kind of excitement, and today everything is supposed to be exciting: vacations, restaurants, music, cars, even breakfast cereals. An attitude of seeking excitement is in the air today, and to me it bodes ill for our civilization if we do not learn how to change. Where people are looking for excitement everywhere, epidemic depression has to follow.

I once saw a newspaper story, for example, about an event billed as one of the most exciting of the season: a "Look Like Greta Garbo" party. Imagine five hundred people paying a fortune to come to a party all looking alike, not only in their costumes but in their wigs, their accents, even their gestures. There must have been weeks of anticipation, planning, rehearsing, fantasizing, talking, dwelling on the pleasure that party would bring. With the Gita's perspective, I had only to read that story to guess that before long the offices of practitioners all over that city would be filled with five hundred look-alike depressives.

Ultimately, it is not overindulging the senses that is the problem in depression; it is indulging our self-will. Whenever we dwell on ourselves – rehearsing pleasure, replaying the past, worrying about getting our way – we are indulging self-will. As far as vitality goes, this is like letting your car sit in the garage all night with the engine idling: you go out in the morning and find that there is no more gas.

All this can be prevented by not wasting prana. Depression – at least the ordinary variety – is an energy crisis. With conservation there is no crisis. When the mind is still, your tank is always full, so you have plenty of vitality for weathering life's ups and downs. The quiet joy of this state is conveyed in precise, simple language by St. Teresa of Avila in one of her rare little poems, stamped with her own experience:

A More Ardent Fire

Her heart is full of joy with love,
For in the Lord her mind is stilled.
Having renounced all selfish attachments,
She draws abiding strength from the One within.
She lives not for herself, but lives
To serve the Lord of Love in all,
And swims across the sea of life
Breasting its rough waves joyfully.

13 *They are pure, efficient, detached,*
ready to meet every demand
I make on them as humble
instruments of my work.

I ONCE KNEW a chap who was an expert at card games, who had a quiet way of making the most of every hand. "A good player," he explained, "can't afford to depend on chance. He's got to be able to play whatever he's dealt." Then he would add, with understandable pride, "Let anybody you like deal the cards – some good, all bad, I don't care. At the end of the evening, I'll still come out on top."

He was talking about cards, but I was thinking, "That's the way to live in freedom too." The word the Gita uses here is *anapeksha,* for which "detached" is a very pale translation. Literally, *anapeksha* means "without expectations." This sounds negative in English, but it is just the opposite. *Anapeksha* means always ready for the unexpected – in other words, ready for anything. This is a very daring attitude. It means telling life, "I'm not concerned with what you send me. Good or bad, pleasant or unpleasant, it doesn't matter; I can make the best of whatever comes."

The opposite of this is not preparedness; it is rigidity. Most of us are subject to this to some degree, and it comes to the surface whenever we have to deal with unexpected problems. From what I have seen of life, problems are a repertory theater. We may be presented with all sorts of characters, but only a few problems are playing all the roles. Self-will, of course, is one of the most versatile. Given a problem that we recognize – dressed in a particular costume, cast in a particular role, appearing at a particular place and time – we know how to deal with it. But the moment the same problem appears in a way we do not expect – say, wearing a false mustache and a fez – we go to pieces. The mind looks through its catalog and throws up its hands: "Boss, this isn't supposed to happen! I don't know what to do."

In other words, to live without expectations is the secret of freedom, especially in personal relationships. There is a song from *My Fair Lady* in which Rex Harrison sings in exasperation:

> Why can't a woman
> Be more like a man?
> . . . .
> Why can't a woman
> Be like *me?*

It did not surprise me to learn that this was a popular song. In every emotional relationship, even if we don't know how to put it into words, each of us has a rigid set of expectations that require the other person to act and think in a particular way. Interestingly enough, it is not that person's way; it is our own. Then, when he or she acts differently, we get surprised and feel irritated or disappointed. If we could see behind the scenes, in the mind, this sort of encounter would make a rather good comedy. Here I am, relating not to you but to my idea of you, and I get irritated because you insist on acting your own way instead!

In the end, this is the basis of most difficulties in personal relationships. It is really no more than stimulus and response. If you behave the way I expect, the way I want, I'll be kind. If you behave otherwise, I'll act otherwise too: rude or irritated or disappointed or depressed, depending on my personality, but always something in reaction to you. It means, very simply, that none of us has much freedom; our behavior is dependent on what other people say and do.

When I first began to observe this in myself, I was astonished. Imagine going through life with handcuffs on and thinking that you're free! Being a college professor, I had always assumed that my intellect did a rather good job. But when I saw that my behavior was nothing but stimulus and response, I looked my intellect in the face and it hung its head. "Look at you," I said, "so well trained, so clever! How is it you couldn't see that my daily living isn't being done by me but by Tom and Dick and Harry?" It was a shocking discovery, but on the other hand, it was a hopeful one. With that discovery came a deep desire to take my life away from that dubious trio and into my own hands.

There is a simple but effective way to do this: give your best everywhere, without reference to anybody else. This frees you from all the vagaries of stimulus and response. On the one hand, by using a passage like this in meditation, you set yourself very high standards of conduct – perhaps the highest that can be imagined. Then you try to apply these standards to everything you do and say and even think throughout the day, without being swayed by anybody else's reaction. If things go your way, you can give your best; if they don't go your way, you can still give your best. All the choices are yours.

In practice, this means that we become the same person always. Most of us think we are the same always, but if we could make objective observations at certain critical times of the day, we would have to conclude that the similarities are on the surface. A mother might say of her pediatrician, "Oh, Dr. Jekyll! He's always so kind, never loses his temper with little Jamie." But his wife or his medical assistant might tell you a different story. "Come see the doctor at home; he's a regular Mr. Hyde."

Most of us are meticulous about how we look when we go out, but we might not mind going about unshaven or with our hair in curlers when we're at home. This is a curious reversal of perspective. I don't want to be at my best only with the mail carrier or the checkout clerk; I want to be at my best always, with everyone, especially with those who are nearest and dearest.

Now, I will be the first to admit that this takes a lot of endurance. When you start giving another person your best, particularly in an emotionally entangled relationship, he may not notice it for weeks. This kind of indifference can really sting. You want to go up to him, tap him on the shoulder, and say, "Hello, George, I've just been kind to you." George would say, "Oh, thank you, I didn't know" — not because he was trying to be rude, but because he was preoccupied with himself. To be patient and go on giving your best, you can't have expectations about how other people are going to respond. You can't afford to ask, "Does he like me or not? I've been putting him first for two whole weeks and I don't think he even cares." What does it matter? If you go on putting him first, he's not the only one who benefits; you're growing.

Especially in a loving relationship, this question of "Does he love me in return?" should not be asked at all. Give the person you love your very best and don't ask about the response. It frees you in your relationship, and it strengthens the other person as well. In one-to-one relationships, most of us tend to lean on each other. If one person wobbles, the other person wobbles too, and sometimes even falls. When you are always at your best, you become a source of strength to those around you. No matter how much they may vacillate, they know they can always lean on you and trust you to stand firm.

If it takes patience to do this in even the best of relationships, it requires real courage in the face of hostile opposition. Here I can make some practical suggestions. For one, concentrate on your own personal conduct. Don't allow your attention to wander to how rude the other person is; concentrate on not being rude yourself. This is terribly difficult, but it frees you to choose your response.

In a sense, this is like the attitude a good athlete has in competition. When the going gets rough, there are some players who get rattled and lose their capacity to concentrate. I have seen a well-known tennis champion lose to a chap who didn't have half his skill, simply because he lost his concentration whenever his challenger got ahead. But some players are actually at their best when they're behind. They don't start worrying about losing and get rattled; they dig in and concentrate even harder on their game. Some of the most brilliant tennis I have seen comes when a fellow like Bjorn Borg fights his way out of a hole against heavy odds to win.

Another suggestion I can offer that used to help me greatly once I caught on to it is this: in an emotionally charged situation, when you find it difficult to concentrate on giving the other person your best, pretend you're an actor on the stage. Play the role of someone who is detached and give your best to your performance.

Let me give a personal example. As a professor I often had to attend faculty meetings, where sparks can really fly. Naturally, when the issue was important to me, I used to express my opinion at those meetings – and as often as not, somebody who felt just as strongly about the opposite view would stand up and take to pieces whatever I had said. Certain people did this with such regularity that the minute they stood up, my adrenal glands would start working overtime, simply because I was about to be contradicted.

Then I began to pretend that instead of being a professor, I was playing the part of a professor: using learned, professorial words, striking certain intellectual attitudes, but all as if it were a role in an off-Broadway performance. If someone contradicted me, my mind could just sit back and watch; it was all part of the play. I even came to enjoy practicing. When my opinions came under fire I would pretend to be Laurence Olivier: take my time to reply, bring the fire of righteous indignation into my eyes, and then state my position in forceful but courteous Victorian English.

Remarkably enough, my colleagues seemed to appreciate this. Two or three went so far as to say, "You know, you've really been making a contribution to these meetings." After all, I felt the same responsibilities as before. I held the same educational concerns. I was simply learning to hold my opinions without rancor in the face of opposition. And where I used to go home after a heated meeting feeling irritated, I now felt like a critic going home after a show. "Much Ado About Nothing again – same cast, modern dress. But not a bad performance from E.E."

People sometimes object, "Isn't this being hypocritical?" Not at all. If anything is hypocritical, it is being angry, behaving rudely, using words calculated to hurt another person. Any kind of negative behavior is untrue to our real Self. When we try to play the role of someone who is kind, we are really learning to be ourselves. There is no need to be afraid of past performances. After all, some of Hollywood's best known "good guys" aren't always such good guys off the screen. Similarly, no matter what you have been like, you can always play a better part, which you will gradually assimilate.

When we quarrel, when we act resentful, that too is a play. It seems natural only because we have rehearsed it so many times. In acting with respect towards others, we are still taking part in the same play, but we have chosen a different role.

Of course, it is difficult to remember this in the heat of the moment, let alone to do it. Even good actors sometimes forget their lines, drop out of character for a moment, and whisper, "What do I say next?" You can do the same. Repeat the mantram and recall these beautiful verses, which meditation will drive deep into your heart: "Pure, efficient, detached, ready to meet every demand I make on them as humble instruments of my work." And then go back to the play. You may not feel the epitome of compassion, but I promise you, you can learn to play the part to perfection.

The marvel of this is that the more often you practice it, the more easily the lines and actions come. After a while they become an integral part of your consciousness.

Some time ago in India there was a play about a great saint, Sri Ramakrishna, which must have been performed all over the country for a number of years. The actor who played the title role, by his own account, was not at all saintly when he took the job. But after years of speaking those inspired lines, taken mostly from Sri Ramakrishna's own words, and acting like a saint night after night, the man's consciousness began to change. He began to want to be a saint. Finally, after the run of the play was over, he gave up acting and devoted himself entirely to the spiritual life.

Ultimately, to give up expectations is to lay aside all the absurd impositions of self-will. Then there is nothing that you require of life; all you want is to give. You have thrown away your defenses. They serve no purpose, for there is nothing life can take away from you. You are always full. In the presence of such a person, others lay down their defenses too.

Many years ago I took my wife and some

friends to see the film version of *Camelot*. One of the younger members of the party was just entering the age when the promises of romance seem eternal, so after the film I asked her what she thought of all those knights. "Oh," she said, "they must have had a very thrilling life. But imagine having to carry around those silly shields!"

Unfortunately, it's not only in Camelot that people carry shields. Virtually all of us labor under defenses that are much more rigid and cumbersome: our expectations. Whenever we feel challenged, we shove these shields up in front of us – and then, when we have trouble relating to others, we complain about bad communication! Even when two people say they are in love with each other, though each may be trying to embrace with one arm, the other arm is still holding on to the same old shield, ready to bring it up again the moment he or she feels a little insecure.

How much vitality is wasted in life by carrying around these shields! They don't even protect us; and as far as relationships go, they constitute most of our problems. The mystics tell us simply, "Throw your shields away." Then we have both arms free to embrace with – in the end, to embrace all life. When we can really embrace with both arms, the message is clear to anyone: "There is nothing I want from you; all I want is to give." This is what all of us are looking for: not only to receive such love but to offer it, freely and consistently, so that our lives will be cherished by everyone around us.

14 *They are dear to me who run not after the pleasant or away from the painful, grieve not over the past, lust not today, but let things come and go as they happen.*

A FRIEND of mine once asked her eight-year-old son what he wanted for Christmas. She was expecting him to say a bicycle or perhaps an electric guitar. His answer took her completely by surprise: "A pair of handcuffs."

When we go through life running after what we like and away from what we dislike, this is just what we are asking for: handcuffs to inhibit every chance of relating to others in freedom. I have met people who were as proud of their handcuffs as that eight-year-old boy. "I'm a man of strong opinions," they say. "I'm a woman who knows what she likes. I'm spontaneous. I'm free." But someone like St.

Francis just gives them a curious smile. "Free, is it? What are those things on your wrists?"

With rare exceptions like St. Francis, this is the conditioning that all of us share: to run after the pleasant and to avoid the unpleasant. It is the old story of stimulus and response. I have read that certain microorganisms, which ordinarily bumble about in random motion, become intentional when particular substances are introduced into their environment. If the substance is pleasant, they move towards it; if it is obnoxious, they move away. I said to myself, "How human!" But there is a crucial difference between us and the rest of creation. As human beings, we have the capacity to decondition ourselves – to train the mind to make the choices that take us beyond conditioned behavior.

The villain here is not actually the mind; it is the ego. The ego has an obsession with taking everything personally. It can't let anything go by without putting in its opinion: "I like this, I don't like that." We may not be aware of it, but if we could listen in on our thoughts, this is the incessant refrain behind all our experience.

When we were living in Oakland we used to go for long walks around the lake, and on Sunday afternoons during the summer we would encounter a band concert. After a while, we began to choose a different hour. It wasn't that I didn't like the music. What I objected to was that there wasn't any choice about listening to it. Wherever you went, you had to be accompanied by John Philip Sousa.

That is the way the ego is. He has a large repertoire of songs and dances, but they all have the same chorus: "I like this, I don't like that." Isn't there a famous choir in which all the singers are boys? Here all the voices are our samskaras, our compulsions. They take every part from soprano to bass, and if they are sometimes squeaky or raucous, they make up for it in enthusiasm. They're willing to practice seven days a week, twenty-four hours a day, as long as we're willing to listen. And the ego is the conductor, standing there with his baton and making sure that everybody comes in on cue.

It is absurd how flimsy likes and dislikes can be. Often, when we meet someone, all it takes to set us off is one little personal characteristic – his nose, her voice, the way he laughs, the way she shows her teeth. Immediately the chorus sets in. And the ego is an excellent conductor. He doesn't have to saw the air; he just lifts his baton and cocks his eyebrows and everybody starts right up: "I don't like it, I don't like it, I don't like it!"

It is pointless to blame the ego for this; it is his nature. If the ego had to declare his identity going through customs, he would say proudly, "I'm a conductor." And if the officials ask, "Is there anybody accompanying you?" I'm sure he would trot out his whole band. "Come on up, boys!" And they would start up right there in the customs shed: "I like this, I don't like that." That is the ego's show, and to paraphrase the Compassionate Buddha, if we hire the ego, we hire the show too.

To put this into practical language, beneath all our liking and disliking is one and the same samskara. A samskara, remember, is a deeply entrenched habit of mind that operates independently of external circumstances. I sometimes compare it to a searchlight: once a searchlight is on, it has to shine, no matter where it is pointing. In this case, we may think we have all sorts of unrelated likes and dislikes – peppermint chip ice cream, hang gliding, names that begin with *A* – but underneath them all is the same old samskara: "I like this, I don't like that."

To take an example, look at procrastination. "I don't like" puts on a fancy costume and calls itself "I have postponed." The disguise can be quite elaborate: "I have all this other urgent work to do," "My other responsibilities just don't leave me time," "I still haven't cleaned out the garage." There may be all sorts of complicating reasons, but underneath, it is often no more than "This isn't pleasant, so I'm not about to do it." That is why Jesus says so often, "Forthwith." If something needs to be done, do it now, without even asking whether it is pleasant or unpleasant. Then you are undoing the samskara, getting rid of your handcuffs.

For a bigger surprise, look at vacillation. Who would think that there is a connection between finding it difficult to make decisions and not being able to love? But as we begin to see the mental states behind behavior, it becomes clear that vacillation has little to do with external circumstances. The mind has simply learned to wobble, and it will wobble back and forth over anything whenever its security is upset.

There is a good word for vacillation in Sanskrit: *chanchala.* It sounds as musical as the bangles on a dancer's ankles, and in Sanskrit poetry a girl with dancing eyes is called *chanchalakshi:* "she whose pupils dart here and there." In the days of classical Indian drama, this was considered a rare attribute. But I see eyes like this every time I go into a supermarket – trying to decide whether to get mint toothpaste or regular, weighing the pros and cons of two brands of soap, wondering whether herbal essence or musk best suits their personalities. People of both sexes are subject to this. They may think they are making independent decisions, but underneath they are asking the same question over and over again: *Do I like this?* It can lead to taking half an hour to decide what kind of toothbrush to buy. "Do I like this? It says it's soft, but there are only two rows of bristles. Or do I like this one? It has three rows, but there's no recommendation by the ADA." We aren't satisfied with selecting one thing and sticking to it; we have to keep asking about it until our attention is dancing all over the store.

The mystics would tell us this has little to do with shopping. It is a habit of mind, and the person who has trouble making decisions in any part of life is going to have trouble making decisions everywhere. In the end, that person will vacillate even in personal relationships. The underlying question is still the same: *Do I like this?* "Do I like him or don't I? He has a nice nose, and I think he likes me, but sometimes I don't care for the way he laughs." When we think this way, every time the other person does something we don't like we stagger a little in our stance. Then he staggers too – we're uncertain, so he's uncertain. It can come to such a state that neither person is able to stand firm; and when that happens in a relationship, life can really be miserable.

In the end, "I don't like" becomes "I can't love." This is why I put so much emphasis on going against likes and dislikes in little things like food. It has really very little to do with food; you're working on the samskara. Enjoying something nourishing that you detest – say, broccoli – may not seem like much of a challenge. But when you learn to eat without rigid attachments, you are really undoing the conditioning of liking and disliking in everything, opening up the handcuffs that keep you from being free.

The problem here, the Gita says, is that our relationships are upside down. We try to build relationships on what is pleasing to us, on physical or emotional attraction. But if there is anything certain about physical attraction, it is that it has to change. We cannot build on it; its very nature is to come and go. To build on a firm foundation, we have to stop asking this question of "What do I like?" and ask only, "What can I give?"

Physical attraction, in other words, is a sensation – here one minute, gone the next. Love is a relationship. It is pleasant to be with someone who is physically attractive, but how long can you enjoy an aquiline nose? How long can you thrill to the timbre of a voice when it doesn't say what you like? It's very much like eating: no matter how much you are attracted to chocolate pie, there is a limit to how much you can enjoy. Beyond that limit, if somebody merely mentions chocolate, your stomach stages a revolt.

That is the most tragic truth about the satisfactions of the senses: they cannot last. It is their nature to come and go, and when the attraction begins to wane, the very things that seemed so pleasant now begin to irritate you. He had such a nice sense of humor when you first met; how is it that his jokes seem corny now? Her smile used to dazzle you; why does she now seem to be all teeth? The wave of passion has risen, now it has to fall: that is all. Pleasure cannot last, any more than the tide can rise without falling again. If you want to build a relationship, don't build it on what changes. Build it on what endures, where the question "Do I like this?" doesn't even arise. Then there is joy in everything, because there is joy in the relationship itself – in ups and downs, through the pleasant and the unpleasant, in sickness and in health.

In Sanskrit, physical attraction is called *kama:* selfish desire, in which I ask only what pleasure I will receive. It is a tremendous force, as we can see from the lives of those with strong passions who are hurled in and out of relationships even against their will. But kama can be transformed – not negated or repressed, but made a matter of free choice, by gradually changing the focus from *me, me, me* to *you, you, you.* Then, in Sanskrit, we say that *kama* becomes *prema:* pure love, where my attention is not on my own pleasure but on the happiness and welfare of those around me.

One of the difficulties in talking about this is that our English word *love* has become almost impossible to use. We talk about a mother's love for her children and mean one thing; we talk about "making love" and mean another. We even talk about loving cheesecake, and we use the phrase "falling in love" as if it were something that could happen every day, like falling into a manhole. Is it so easy to fall in love? We have to learn to love, and it takes a lot of time and a lot of effort.

Listen to our popular songs; look at our magazines and newspapers. When they say "I love you," that's not what I hear; I hear "I love me." If we could listen in on a marriage proposal with the ears of St. Francis, this is what we would hear. The man gets down on bended knee and says, "Sibyl dear, I love me; will you marry me?" You'll make me happy, so won't you marry me? And Sibyl, who is nobody's fool, says, "I love me too – and you'll make *me* happy. So I will."

To be honest, there is a little undertone of this in the relationships of almost all of us. There is no need to be ashamed of it: this is how we have been conditioned, to put ourselves first at least some of the time. But where I like to place emphasis is on the fact that all of us can change. Every relationship begins like this to some extent: some passionate *I love you*'s and some undertones of *I love me*. But if you want your relationship to blossom, you won't dwell on each other's weaknesses. You'll set to work to correct them together and really learn how to love.

I wish I could convey what unending artistry there is in this challenge – artistry and satisfaction and lasting joy. Every day we should be able to love more than the day before. Otherwise there is no growth, which means that things are getting pretty dull. Every day the same old story, "I love you with all my heart"? It may be enough for the romance magazines, but it's not enough for a mystic.

Look at our travel ads: "Experience the Bahamas." How gullible we can be! They show us a couple of swaying palms, some azure waters lapping at white sands, and then they ask innocently, "Wouldn't you like to sit beneath these coconut palms and fall in love?" I come from Kerala, the "land of the coconut palm," and you can take it from me: never try to pursue your dreams beneath a coconut tree. Coconuts have a way of falling on romantic heads, and even the smallest nut, if it drops from a height of fifty feet, can put an end to your romance before it starts. What do swaying palms and azure waters have to do with love? Love doesn't need an exotic setting; it can flourish in the kitchen, in the garden, wherever two people are putting each other first.

If you want to know what love is, look at a woman who knows how to be patient when her husband is irritated. Instead of fanning his mood, she strengthens him by bearing with him until his mind quiets down. In my book, that woman is a great lover. Or look at a man who comes home after work instead of going to a bar, who plays with his children even though he's tired, stays and talks with his wife while they do the dishes instead of flopping down by himself in front of the TV. He is a great lover, even if you never see his name on the Hollywood marquees.

When you live with a person like this, the time will come when you find it impossible even to think a harsh thought about each other. You may not completely understand each other, you may not always see eye to eye, but each of you will know without doubt that the other's loyalty will never waver. When this happens, you are no longer living in Berkeley or San Francisco. It is paradise, "Jerusalem's green land," right here on earth. There may be differences on the surface, but underneath the surface there is only pure, selfless love.

Two people like this are no longer really two; they are one. When things are sunny, you may not notice how their relationship shines. But wait until the storms begin to blow outside, when everything is going wrong: you will see unfailing support between them, unfaltering loyalty, tenderness that never ends. "Call it not love that changes": it is wise advice. This is the pinnacle of love, and nothing less can ever satisfy us.

15 *Who serve both friend and foe*
with equal love, not buoyed up
by praise nor cast down by blame,
alike in heat and cold, pleasure
and pain, free from selfish attach-
ments and self-will, ever full, in
harmony everywhere, firm in
faith – such as these are dear
to me.

I DON'T THINK anyone illustrates these verses better than Mahatma Gandhi, for whom love and selfless action were one. "I don't want to be at home only with my friends," he said. "I want to be at home with my enemies too." It wasn't a manner of speaking; he lived it out through forty years of solid opposition.

I have seen newsreel footage of Gandhi with a prominent political figure who opposed him so relentlessly that people said he had a problem for every solution Gandhi offered. These scenes were shot in 1944, when the two leaders met for a series of talks in which literally millions of lives were hanging in the balance. It took my breath away to see Gandhi treating his opponent with the affection one shows an intimate friend. At the beginning of each day's discussions the man's face would be a mask of hostility; at the end of the day both men would come out together smiling and joking. Then by the next morning the man would have frozen over again, and Gandhi would start all over with the same cheerful patience, trying to find some common ground.

That is how the mystic approaches conflict, and it pulls the rug out from under the traditional theories. There is a lot being written these days about conflict resolution, which I am glad to see. But generally they will say, in effect, "This is how you deal with your opponent." Gandhi, St. Francis, St. Teresa, would all say, "No. The moment you start thinking about the other person as an opponent, you make it impossible to find a solution." There are no opponents in a disagreement; there are simply two people facing a common problem. In other words, they are not in opposite camps. They are in the same camp: the real opponent is the problem.

To apply this, you have to set aside the question of who is to blame. We have a saying in my mother tongue: "It takes two to get married and it takes two to quarrel." No matter what the circumstances, neither person bears sole responsibility for a quarrel. This is an encouraging outlook, because if both are responsible, both together can find a solution – not merely a compromise, but a way actually to resolve the disagreement peacefully.

To do this, however, it is necessary to listen – and listen with respect. Don't be afraid if the other person is angry. An angry person is blind. He is so absorbed in his own point of view that he cannot see what is happening around him, including what is happening to himself. We don't get angry with those who are blind; we help them: after all, unless they have taught themselves to be extraordinarily sensitive with their other faculties, blind people can bump into things and hurt themselves and others. That is just how an angry person is; and when we have to face such people, we need to listen with patience and respect and help them not to rush off blindly into a lamp post. Whether the other person is polite or not, the objective is still the same: how can we find the common point of view?

Here the mystics ask a simple but subtle question: how can you end a quarrel if you do not even hear what the quarrel is about? How can you solve a problem with two sides if you never hear what the other side is? More than that, if you can't listen to the other person with detachment, you will not have the detachment to understand your own position objectively either. It's not just one side of the problem you can't see; it's both. So listen with respect: it may hurt you, it may irritate you, but it is a healing process.

Gradually, if you can bear with this, you will find that you are no longer thinking about "my point of view" and "your point of view." Instead you say, "There is a point of view that is common to you and me, which we can discover together." Once you can do this, the quarrel is over. You may not yet have arrived at a solution – usually, in fact, there is a lot of hard work left to do. But the quarrel itself is over, because now you know that there are two of you playing on the same side against the problem.

I remember watching the Brazilian athlete Pelé play his last game of soccer. He was retiring at the peak of his career, probably the best soccer player the world has seen, and in his final match he was playing with the New York Cosmos against the team for which he had scored his most memorable goals: Santos of Brazil. For the first half of the game, Pelé played his best for the Cosmos. But the second half had a brilliant touch: he joined Santos and played his best for *them.* This is what we should do in a disagreement: play half-time for the other side, half-time for our own. It is not a question of sacrificing principles; this is the only way to see the whole.

If we could only see the game more clearly – and the results were not so tragic – the spectacle of a quarrel would make us laugh. When we played soccer in my village, one of my cousins used to get so excited that he would shoot the ball into his own goal. We used to say, "Never mind the other side; watch out for Mandan." When two people quarrel, that's just what they are doing – scoring against their own side. Whatever the disagreement, we are the Home Team, the Cosmos – all of us. Our problems, whether personal or national or environmental, are the Visitors. And the mystics say simply, "Support your team. There is the opponent, down at the other end of the field. Unite against the problem; don't go scrapping among yourselves."

Otherwise, if I may say so, there are no winners in this game. Once we divide against ourselves, whether at home or between races or nations, there can only be losers.

On the other hand, there is no disagreement so serious that it cannot be set right if both sides can get together and work hard for a common solution. It is not at all easy, and the results will not be immediate. But wherever there is hatred, complete love can be established; wherever there is conflict, complete unity can be established. The choice is up to us.

Jesus puts it perfectly: "Love your enemies." You will never see any loftier words, but never any more practical either, for he is telling us how to rise to our highest stature. Look at the sun, he says; does it shine only on those it likes? It shines on all, it gives to all; and we should learn to love the way the sun shines, without favor or interruption. Bless them that curse you; do good to them that hate you. In time they may learn to love you, but that is not the point. What *we* are called on to do is to be at our best always.

There is room for great artistry in this – especially when it is not on a grand scale, as it was for Gandhi, but in the everyday life of home and work.

Here, I think, no one provides a finer example than St. Thérèse of Lisieux:

> In our community there is a Sister who has a talent for displeasing me in everything. Her ways, her words, her character seem to me very disagreeable. However, she is a holy Sister whom the good Lord must find quite agreeable. So, not wanting to give in to the natural antipathy I was feeling, I told myself that charity must consist not in sentiments but in action. Then I applied myself to do for this Sister just what I would do for the person I love most . . . I tried to render her every possible service, and when I was tempted to answer her in a disagreeable way, I contented myself with giving her my friendliest smile and tried to change the subject. As she was absolutely ignorant of how I felt for her, . . . she told me one day with a contented air, almost in these very words: "Would you tell me, Sister Thérèse, what attracts you so much towards me? Each time you see me I see you smiling." Ah! What attracts me is Jesus, hidden in the depths of her soul – Jesus who makes sweet that which is most bitter. . . . I answered that I was smiling because I was pleased to see her. (Of course, I didn't add that it was from the spiritual point of view!)

In a small way, this is something that every sincere spiritual aspirant must go through in order to learn to love. In my own life, I too had to deal with people who disliked me – and, I have to confess, I did not care for them either. But as meditation deepened, I began to understand: that was the challenge of it. As Jesus asks, "Where is the achievement in loving those who like you? Anybody can do that."

If you're daring, this is a challenge that can appeal deeply. After all, if you really want to play championship tennis, you won't want to play against people like me. You'll say, "Put me across the net from Chris Evert or Jimmy Connors. Even if I lose, the game is going to be worthwhile."

Once I got that perspective, I really joined battle with my likes and dislikes where relationships were concerned. If there was someone I had always avoided, who always avoided me, I gritted my teeth and began to try to win him over. The first few times, my knees were shaking as if somebody had given me a pair of boxing gloves and put me in the ring with Muhammad Ali. And sometimes, at the beginning, I was knocked down. But I wasn't depressed: even if I hadn't laid a glove on my samskara, I had made it through the first round. That itself was a triumph and a revelation. I wanted to cheer, to pat my mind on the back and say, "Never mind about winning or losing. At least we know that now we can make a fight of it. We don't have to give up and be knocked out by the very first blow." I felt as if all my chains had been broken, and if I had been the uninhibited kind, I would have got up and danced like Zorba the Greek. And after that, if a desire to retaliate or speak harshly came up, I would fight it with all I had.

It hurt. After all, I was a professor of the English language. I knew how to use words, I had a large vocabulary at my disposal, and sometimes all sorts of choice remarks would rush to my tongue and pile up behind my teeth, clamoring to get out. But no matter how much pain it caused, I wouldn't speak until I could make my point in calm, courteous language that would not hurt the person who had hurt me.

Sometimes, after a lot of patient effort, I was successful in winning over such people. But sometimes, though I tried my level best, I was not. It was terribly disheartening. At times I was tempted to ask myself, "Wasn't all that effort wasted? All that time you spent with that person, listening to him, walking with him, playing tennis with him, when you could have been reading the mystics?" But then I looked again. I hadn't lost a thing – and I had made myself so secure that I could flourish in any relationship and never be let down.

"Be ye therefore perfect," Jesus says, "even as thy Father in heaven." That is the goal, nothing less. Why ask if it is possible? It doesn't matter; we can always move towards perfection. In India – I imagine the same is true all over the world – children like to measure their height each year with a little mark on a wall. We can do the same: take a few minutes to take stock of our day and see how we can improve. Don't psychologize or dwell on major failures. Two or three minutes morning or evening should be enough to take a bird's-eye view of landmark events and look for ways in which you can do better on the next day. When you came to breakfast, were you a little abrupt? Did you get caught up in a silent dialogue with your oatmeal? Make a point of being especially attentive the following day. Was there somebody at work to whom – perhaps unintentionally – you gave a cold shoulder?

Next day make it warm. That is all – little things. Life consists of these little things, and it is by putting other people first every day in a thousand small acts of kindness that we make ourselves perfect in love.

There are people, I am told, who examine their faces every evening for signs of advancing age. I would say, don't look for crow's-feet on the surface; turn the mirror inwards. Take a detached look, shake your finger at the mirror, and tell yourself, "Watch out! You think you did pretty well today – but tomorrow I'm going to be even more patient; I'm going to love even more."

If you want to love with all your heart, this is the key: don't ever ask how much you can get; ask how much you can give. It is applicable everywhere.

Some time ago I saw a very accomplished actor, Paul Scofield, in a film of one of Shakespeare's finest plays, *King Lear*. The tragedy is relentless, and it can tear your heart to hear old Lear, in the twilight of his life, trying to bolster himself with attestations of his daughters' love: "Regan, how much do you love me? Goneril, how much do you love me?" I had only to hear those lines to foresee that terrible moment when Lear cries out to the gathering storm,

> You see me here, you gods, a poor old man,
> As full of grief as age.

I am no longer an English professor; my entire life is devoted to teaching meditation. But if I could make a sally back into the world of letters, I could write a very different version of that play. I wouldn't write a tragedy. Lear would learn to change his whole way of thinking. It would all be "Goneril, how much can I love you? Regan, how can I love you more?" And at the end of the play, instead of huddling on the moors buffeted by the winter weather, he would stand erect and tell the sky, "Look upon a man as full of love as he is of age." *That* is King Lear; the other was a pauper. It can be true of all of us: the power to rewrite is in our hands.

"If you want to know how good a person is," the mystics say, "ask how much he loves." It is a perfect epigram, but I like to turn it around. If you want to test the depth of someone's love, look at how kind he is, how patient she is – not when things are going smoothly, but in their hours of trial. A ship isn't tested in a harbor; it's tested on the high seas. There are great scientists, artists, philosophers, soldiers, who function well enough when life is with them but go to pieces when the storms begin to blow. And the mystics say, "Set aside the goal of life, set aside meditation; what good is a ship that's only seaworthy in port?" Look at the daring of a great lover like Gandhi or St. Teresa. When somebody opposes them, instead of running away, they move closer; when someone is angry with them, they try all the harder to be kind.

Love "has no errors," says William Law, "for all errors are the want of love." When we have problems in our relationships, it is not that love has failed; these are defects in our ability to love. In our contemporary climate of separateness, it has become almost impossible for a man and woman to remain together for more than a short period of time. But to throw up our hands and say that love won't work, that lasting relationships are no longer possible, simply betrays our ignorance of what love means.

I read a lot these days about the decline in literacy. But when it comes to love, virtually all of us are illiterates. This is not a condemnation. When you were two, did you know how to read? And even when you began to learn, wasn't it mostly things like "See Spot run"? There is no need to be embarrassed about this; that is how all of us began. To read a writer like Shakespeare with real understanding takes most of us twenty years – and even then we may not be able to follow the simple words of John of the Cross when he soars into realms where we have never been.

It is the same with love. At the outset, it is wise to admit freely that this is an art that we do not know. But we can put ourselves to school; and if we are willing to put in at least the time it takes to understand Shakespeare, all of us can become perfect in love.

When two people love each other, there is one sure sign: they want to lose themselves in their unity. These are simple words, but the more you reflect on them and try to practice them, the more you will see how profound a concept this is, how difficult to practice. It is just the opposite of what we hear around us: "Maintain your individuality, maintain your own little separate personality, and then try to get along together as best you can." In the Gita's terms, this is the denial of love. Each person is drawing a little circle around himself or herself and saying, "I will function freely in my circle; you can function freely in yours." The circles do not even overlap, which means there is no real relationship between those people at all.

This is how we begin. Most of us, if we could see objectively, stand inside virtually separate circles, which we ourselves have drawn. That is what self-will does. To move closer, we need to reduce self-will. It is difficult, distressing, even dangerous; that is its challenge. But gradually, as self-will decreases, the circles you and your partner have drawn around yourselves move closer together, until at last they touch.

After that, the work is equally strenuous. Now you try to make the circles overlap, so that each intersects a little arc. During eight hours together, you try to preserve at least one hour when there is no acrimony, no competition, no selfishness. For the other seven hours, your mind may have been complaining bitterly. It's quite all right: there is now an arc in common. Vast areas remain that need to come together, but you can concentrate on that little area of unity and say, "Yes, it is possible. Even if it takes years, these circles *can* become one."

If we could but see it, there are not many separate circles; there is only one. All have the same center and the same radius; nobody's area is different from anybody else's. You may have been born in Rhodesia and your partner in Rhode Island – two different environments, different languages, different cultures – but there is not the slightest difference between the Self in you and the Self in him or her. This is the realization that comes in Self-realization. All circles merge, and afterwards you don't see separate circles at all. Love is playing like a perpetual fountain in your heart: love not for only one person but for all people, all creatures, all forms of life.

The closer two people grow, the deeper is the longing to become closer still. But nothing short of absolute unity is going to fulfill the deep, driving need in the heart of every one of us to be one and indivisible. Even in the most passionate Romeo-and-Juliet relationship there will always be a void, a hunger that can be satisfied only for a short while. Pick up the paper almost any morning and you will find somebody complaining that this satisfaction has come to an end. "We're together all week long; I need a vacation from him." "She's always there when I come home; I need one evening a week all to myself." I read recently about two people trying to preserve their relationship by seeing each other only on weekends. I wanted to ask, "What relationship is there to preserve?" If the object is to keep life from becoming humdrum, why not just have a breathless encounter once a year when your paths cross in the air terminal at St. Paul?

When two people really love each other, they will want to be together always. It is one of the surest tests of love. It doesn't mean becoming dependent on each other, or sitting together on a love seat writing sonnets. It means working together in a selfless cause, merging two lives into a single, beneficial force. When you have a relationship like that, even a hundred years together would not satisfy you. If you can be satisfied by anything that is limited, your love is not complete. When your two circles come together you will cry, with the daring of the mystic, "Let there be no separation."

In the spiritual tradition of India, we have a story that illustrates this beautifully. There was a girl who was born of highly spiritual parents. At school she had many friends among the other girls, and gradually, as they reached the age for marriage, she began to come home with wonderful news. "Mummy," she would say, "Nalini is going to get married! You know Nalini, the one who always wears jasmine in her hair. She is going to get married, and her mother is getting her a beautiful new sari, and she'll be exchanging garlands and wearing new jewelry . . ."

And her mother, who knew how to read the mixed look of joy and longing in her daughter's eyes, would smile and say, "Be happy for her."

This happened year after year, until at last our little girl had grown into her late teens. Finally, on the day of her graduation, she came home crying as if her heart would break. "Mummy," she said, "all the girls in my class are married now! I saw their faces shining at the wedding, and now I don't see them any more. Their lives are joyful – and look at me; I don't think I'm going to be married at all."

The mother, who was a woman of great spiritual stature, did not try to answer immediately. She took her daughter into the meditation room, sat down with her, and taught her how to meditate. Then she explained, "These marriages you have seen were good; but in life, the sunshine is always mixed with shadow. There are days that are sweet, but there are also days that are bitter: and after this play of light and shadow, sweet and bitter, has gone on for many years, time itself is going to bring the relationship to an end."

"Is there no marriage that is perfect?" the daughter asked. "Is there no relationship that lasts, that has no end?"

"There is," her mother said. "It *is* possible to love forever; but it is terribly, terribly hard."

"That's what I want," the girl pleaded. "That is what I have been longing for all these years, and to love like that, I am prepared to give up everything else."

"Then give all your love, your heart, your time, your life, to serve the Lord of Love. Offer him everything: 'whatever you do, whatever you enjoy, even what you suffer,' do it only for him. Make your whole life a gift to him, and you will be united with him by a love that time can never bring to an end." She looks at her daughter, so eager and so strong, and asks: "Are you able to do all this?"

And the girl, now grown far beyond her years, answers simply, "I am." Like little Thérèse Martin, like other great teenagers in the Indian scriptures, she devotes herself completely to the overriding goal of going beyond change and death. And the story tells beautifully – almost in the same language that Catholic mystics use – that at last, Sri Krishna comes to her in the depths of her consciousness and accepts her as his eternal bride. *"Amado con amada,"* writes John of the Cross, *"Amada en el amado transformada"* – lover with the Beloved, united, transfigured, transformed.

16 *But even dearer are those who seek me in faith and love as life's one supreme goal. They go beyond death to eternal life.*

IN THE Rig Veda, one of the most ancient of the Hindu scriptures, there is a prayer that still finds a response in every heart:

> Lead me from the unreal to the real,
> Lead me from darkness to light,
> Lead me from death to immortality.

This is the central theme of mysticism in all religions: the quest for deathlessness, for everlasting life.

Until I took to the practice of meditation, it never occurred to me that immortality could be any more than a figure of speech – a rhetorical device that can strengthen and inspire us, but nothing that could be literally true. It was only by observing my Granny's attitude towards death that I began to understand that the quest for deathlessness was real: a living search that any person with drive and enthusiasm could undertake, not after death but in this very life. In both East and West there have been rare men and women who have been enabled through spiritual disciplines to transcend the conditioning of time, place, and the physical body. For people like this, there is no death. The body dies, of course; but there is no interruption of consciousness when the body falls away, because their identification with the body has already been severed.

In deep meditation, when consciousness is withdrawn from the body and senses, there actually come a few moments when you go beyond the body. The five buttons of the body-jacket, the senses, are undone, and for a short while you are able to slip your arms out, hang up your jacket in the meditation room, and rest in your real nature. That is a taste of immortality right on earth, and there is such joy in it, such a deep sense of peacefulness and rest, that afterwards you will be willing to give everything to extend those moments into the full twenty-four hours of the day.

Once that is done, the ties of identification with the body are severed once and for all. You know at the deepest level that you are not the body but the soul, the Self, and when death comes, it is simply a matter of hanging up this particular jacket for the last time. As al-Ghazali asks, where is the cause for grief in this? Is consciousness ruptured when you take off your shirt at night?

There are no words to describe this state, but the mystics of all religions say quietly, "It's like waking up." Before the realization of God, we are living in our sleep – dreaming that we are separate fragments of life, small enough to be satisfied with wisps of experience that come and go. Aren't the experiences of a dream real while we are dreaming? In a vivid dream, there is at best only a hazy memory of another state of consciousness to which we can awaken. Yet when we do wake up again, the dream falls away. And the mystics ask a very simple question: when you have been dreaming that you are Marco Polo, ranging all over the world into distant lands, and you wake up, are you a different person? Do you grieve that Marco Polo is gone? He isn't gone: you were dreaming that you were he; now you wake up, the dream is forgotten, and you remember who you really are.

In the Katha Upanishad, there is a daring teenager named Nachiketa who goes straight to the King of Death for the secret of immortality. "I have heard," he tells Death, "from the illumined sages that there is a kingdom where you never come, where one lives free from death in everlasting joy." There *is* such a kingdom, but it is not outside us. In the early part of our lives, most of us are off on an external journey, looking for Shangri-la in the lands of the senses. But to those who are sensitive, there comes more and more insistently a sense of homesickness, of being wanderers on the earth; and finally there comes a point where we throw aside all the travel brochures of the sense-world and turn inwards to find our real home. Then the quest for deathlessness begins in earnest.

This is a demanding, arduous, challenging journey. As meditation deepens and we get beneath the surface level, we see a wholly different world within us: the world of the unconscious, as vast as the world outside us, without boundaries in time or space. Gerard Manley Hopkins gives a glimpse of these realms in a tortuous poem:

> O the mind, mind has mountains; cliffs of fall
> Frightful, sheer, no-man-fathomed. Hold them
>   cheap
> May who ne'er hung there....

To those who live on the surface of life, the dangers of this world seem "cheap," insignificant. But once we glimpse the scope of the unconscious, it can take our breath away. Hopkins is not exercising poetic license; these mountains and cliffs and gorges are as real as those beneath the surface of the sea. To make a journey like this, it is not enough to have courage and determination. We should also have some idea of where we are going.

I remember a book with an intriguing title: *If You Don't Know Where You're Going, You'll Probably End Up Somewhere Else.* We already *are* somewhere else; our need now is to get back home. A life goal is like a polestar: you can guide your whole journey by it. You may take detours or wrong turns, but if you keep your eyes on the goal, you will always be able to know when you are off course and how to get back again. Without a goal there can only be wandering; with a goal you can never get lost. And the Lord says here, "Don't settle for anything outside you. Make me your only goal."

Years ago my little friend Rama received a picture puzzle of an elephant, and when I came into the living room I found pieces strewn all over the floor. I grew up among elephants, so I thought I would be able to recognize an elephant from any conceivable angle. But no amount of looking at those pieces enabled me to distinguish head from tail. Then Rama showed me the picture on the box. After that, even though it might take a long time and a lot of trial and error, I knew I would be able to make those pieces into an elephant if I tried.

This is what we do in meditation. I would suggest memorizing this chapter of the Bhagavad Gita, "The Way of Love," and using it regularly in meditation. (You will find it at the end of this book, translated especially for use in meditation.) There is no more inspiring portrait by which to arrange the pieces of our lives. As you travel deeper into consciousness, these verses will shape your daily living; even in your sleep you will want to realize them. "Free from selfish attachments and self-will, ever full, in harmony everywhere . . ." At the beginning these are only inspiring words, describing someone like Mahatma Gandhi or St. Teresa. But after many years of meditation and the allied disciplines, when this ideal has been completely integrated into your consciousness, it will be in a small way a portrait of yourself: not the little self with which you identified when you began this journey, but a person who has been transformed, reborn, remade in the image of this all-consuming ideal.

In the final stages of this journey, it is necessary to use all kinds of contradictions to describe what is happening within you. Everything is coming together, your desires are almost unified; and when you sit down for meditation, you drop like a plummet into the very depths of consciousness. In some strange way, you expect without expecting. You wait impatiently, yet you are prepared to wait a hundred years. Every day you give your very best in your meditation, your work, your personal relationships, so that nothing will delay this tremendous climax. And in the evening too you stay vigilant, keeping the mantram going ceaselessly; for as

Jesus warns, "Ye know not what hour thy Lord may come"; he may come like a thief in the night.

In these final stages there can be deep experiences in your sleep, experiences that are preparing the way for the climax of Self-realization. You may hear the mantram reverberating through your consciousness, or the words of a passage you have been using in meditation. You may see one of the great spiritual figures you love deeply, or even have a vision of Jesus or Sri Krishna or the Compassionate Buddha. It is like the curtain trying to go up on a play you have been waiting for all your life. You can see the feet of the stagehands, you know that the sets are being moved into place, but that is all; and it so inflames your eagerness that you exclaim, like India's great mystic and poet Meera,

> Oh, how I long to see my Lord!
> At dawn I search for him
> Every day in my meditation;
> I cannot sleep until my eyes behold him.
> Ages have I been separated from you, Beloved!
> When will you come?

This is not the experience of a few days. It can go on for months, even years, and it is the most deliciously difficult period in the search for God. No mystic would ever be spared that agony. There is such joy in it that the Sufis ask, how much more joy must there be in the final union, when all separateness comes to an end? Then, says Abu Said in rapture, "I am lover, Beloved, and love in one; beauty and mirror and the eyes that see." Jafar exclaims:

I have joined my heart to thee: all that exists
    art thou.
O Lord, beloved of my heart, thou art the
    home of all;
Where indeed is the heart in which thou dost not
    dwell? . . .
From earth below to the highest heaven, from
    heaven to deepest earth,
I see thee wherever I look: all that exists art thou.

When we are united with the Lord, every created thing, from the farthest star to the atoms in our bodies, is our kith and kin. Remember William Blake looking at the sun and seeing a choir of angels singing "Holy, holy, holy"? The whole of creation is singing; if we cannot hear it, it is simply because we are asleep.

When I was growing up at the feet of my grandmother, though I loved her passionately, I understood very little of her perspective. My attention was elsewhere, on Shakespeare and Dickens and the "Ode to a Nightingale"; I couldn't hear what her life was proclaiming every instant – in the simple words of St. Angela, almost the same as those of the Gita, "the whole world is full of God."

There is no barrier between us and this realization except self-will. That is all that keeps us thinking that we are separate from the whole. The more we love, the less our self-will – and the less subject we are to time and death. All of us have moments when we forget ourselves in helping others. In those moments of self-forgetfulness, we step out of ourselves: we really cease, if only for an instant, to be a separate person. Those are moments of immortality, right on earth. Stretch them out until they fill the day and you will no longer be living in yourself alone; you will live in everyone. And St. John of the Cross reminds us, "We live in what we love." If you love the Lord in all, if you live in the Lord in all, what is there to die when the body dies?

On her deathbed, St. Thérèse of Lisieux was asked what she thought heaven would be like. Thérèse replied in her gentle way that she couldn't imagine it would be so very different. "Oh, I know I'll see God. But as for being in his presence, I couldn't be more so there than I am here."

Perfect words. When the little prison of the ego has been left behind, there is no longer any real difference between "there" and "here." We no longer live in a separate body, a separate little personality. The whole universe is our home.

Sri Sarada Devi, mourning for Sri Ramakrishna on the evening after he died, heard him ask in the depths of her consciousness: "Am I dead, that you are acting like a widow? I have only moved from one room to another." And the Compassionate Buddha, in one of the most magnificent passages in mystical literature anywhere, chooses almost the same image:

In vain have I gone around these countless cycles of birth and death, looking for the builder of this house. How wearisome is the suffering of being born again and again! But now I have seen you, housebuilder; you shall not build this house of separateness again. The rafters are broken, the ridgepole has been destroyed: I have gone beyond all selfish craving; I have attained nirvana, in which all sorrows end.

PART FOUR

An Eight-Point Program

An Eight-Point Program

WHEN I came to this country as an exchange professor in 1959, I was invited to speak to many groups of people on the sources of India's ancient civilization. At the end of every talk a few thoughtful men and women would come up and ask me, "How can we bring these changeless values into our own daily life?"

"You don't have to change your religion," I assured them, "to do what I have done. The method of meditation I learned is universal. It can be practiced within the mainstream of any religious tradition, and outside all of them as well."

I began by teaching simply what I myself had been practicing for over a decade, illustrating from the scriptures and mystics of the world's great religions. Very quickly this became systematized into eight points, the first and most important of which is meditation. The next few pages are a short introduction to this eight-point program for spiritual growth, which is discussed fully in my book *Meditation*.

1. Meditation

The heart of this program is meditation: half an hour every morning, as early as is convenient. Do not increase this period; if you want to meditate more, have half an hour in the evening also, preferably at the very end of the day.

Set aside a room in your home to be used only for meditation and spiritual reading. After a while that room will become associated with meditation in your mind, so that simply entering it will have a calming effect. If you cannot spare a room, have a particular corner. Whichever you choose, keep your meditation place clean, well ventilated, and reasonably austere.

Sit in a straight-backed chair or on the floor and gently close your eyes. If you sit on the floor, you may need to support your back against a wall. You should be comfortable enough to forget your body, but not so comfortable that you become drowsy.

Whatever position you choose, be sure to keep your head, neck, and spinal column erect in a straight line. As concentration deepens, the nervous system relaxes and you may begin to fall asleep. It is important to resist this tendency right from the beginning, by drawing yourself up and away from your back support until the wave of sleep has passed.

Once you have closed your eyes, begin to go slowly, in your mind, through one of the passages from the scriptures or the great mystics which I recommend for use in meditation. There is a rich selection in my little anthology, *God Makes the Rivers to Flow.* I usually suggest learning first the Prayer of St. Francis of Assisi:

Lord, make me an instrument of thy peace.
Where there is hatred, let me sow love;
Where there is injury, pardon;
Where there is doubt, faith;
Where there is despair, hope;
Where there is darkness, light;
Where there is sadness, joy.

O divine master, grant that I may not so
   much seek
To be consoled as to console;
To be understood as to understand;
To be loved as to love;
For it is in giving that we receive;
It is in pardoning that we are pardoned;
It is in dying to self that we are born to eternal life.

In memorizing the prayer, it is important to remember that you are not addressing some extraterrestrial being outside you. The kingdom of heaven is within us, and the Lord is enshrined in the depths of our own consciousness. When we use a prayer like this, we are calling deep into ourselves, appealing to the spark of the divine that is our real nature.

While you are meditating, do not follow any association of ideas or try to think about the passage. If you are giving your attention to each word, the meaning cannot help sinking in. When distractions come, do not resist them, but give more attention to the words of the passage. If your mind strays from the passage entirely, bring it back gently to the beginning and start again.

When you reach the end of the passage, you may use it again as necessary to complete your period of meditation until you have memorized others. It is helpful to have a wide variety of passages for meditation, drawn from the world's major traditions. Each passage should be positive and practical, drawn from a major scripture or from a mystic of the highest stature.

The secret of meditation is simple: we become what we meditate on. When you use the Prayer of St. Francis every day in meditation, you are driving the words deep into your consciousness. Eventually they become an integral part of your personality, which means they will find constant expression in what you do, what you say, and what you think.

2. The Mantram or Holy Name

A mantram, or Holy Name, is a powerful spiritual formula that has the capacity to transform consciousness when it is repeated silently in the mind. There is nothing magical about this. It is simply a matter of practice, as you can verify for yourself.

Every religious tradition has a mantram, often more than one. For Christians, the name of Jesus itself is a powerful mantram. Catholics also use *Hail Mary* or *Ave Maria*, or some form of the Jesus Prayer preserved in the Orthodox church, such as *Lord, Jesus Christ, have mercy on us.* Jews may use *Barukh attah Adonai*, "Blessed art thou, O Lord," or the Hasidic formula *Ribono shel olam*, "Lord of the universe." Muslims repeat the name of Allah or *Allahu akbar*, "God is great." Probably the oldest of Buddhist mantrams is *Om mani padme hum*, referring to the "jewel in the lotus of the heart." In Hinduism, among many choices, I recommend *Rama, Rama, Rama*, the mantram used by Mahatma Gandhi.

Select a mantram that appeals to you deeply. In many traditions it is customary to take the mantram used by your spiritual teacher. Then, once you have chosen, do not change your mantram. Otherwise you will be like a person digging shallow holes in many places; you will never go deep enough to find water.

Repeat your mantram silently whenever you get the chance: while walking, while waiting, while you are doing mechanical chores like washing dishes, and especially when you are falling asleep. You will find for yourself that this is not mindless repetition. The mantram will help to keep you relaxed and alert during the day, and when you can fall asleep in it, it will go on working for you throughout the night as well.

Whenever you are angry or afraid, nervous or worried or resentful, repeat the mantram until the agitation subsides. The mantram works to steady the mind, and all these emotions are power running against you which the mantram can harness and put to work.

These and many other ways to use the mantram are illustrated in my little book *The Mantram Handbook*.

3. Slowing Down

Hurry makes for tension, insecurity, inefficiency, and superficial living. I believe that it also makes for illness: among other things, "hurry sickness" is a major component of the Type A behavior pattern that research has linked to heart disease. To guard against hurrying through the day, start the day early and simplify your life so that you do not try to fill your time with more than you can do. When you find yourself beginning to speed up, repeat your mantram to help you slow down.

It is important here not to confuse slowness with sloth, which breeds carelessness, procrastination, and general inefficiency. In slowing down we should attend meticulously to details, giving our very best even to the smallest undertaking.

4. One-Pointed Attention

Doing more than one thing at a time divides attention and fragments consciousness. When we read and eat at the same time, for example, part of our mind is on what we are reading and part on what we are eating; we are not getting the most from either activity. Similarly, when talking with someone, give him or her your full attention. These are little things, but all together they help to unify consciousness and deepen concentration.

Everything we do should be worthy of our full attention. When the mind is one-pointed it will be secure, free from tension, and capable of the concentration that is the mark of genius in any field.

5. *Training the Senses*

In the food we eat, the books and magazines we read, the movies we see, all of us are subject to the conditioning of rigid likes and dislikes. To free ourselves from this conditioning, we need to learn to change our likes and dislikes freely when it is in the best interests of those around us or ourselves. We should choose what we eat by what our body needs, for example, rather than by what the taste buds demand. Similarly, the mind eats too, through the senses. In this age of mass media, we need to be particularly discriminating in what we read and what we choose for entertainment, for we become in part what our senses take in.

6. *Putting Others First*

Dwelling on ourselves builds a wall between ourselves and others. Those who keep thinking about their needs, their wants, their plans, their ideas cannot help becoming lonely and insecure. The simple but effective technique I recommend is to learn to put other people first – beginning within the circle of your family and friends, where there is already a basis of love on which to build. When husband and wife try to put each other first, for example, they are not only moving closer to each other. They are also removing the barriers of their ego-prison, which deepens their relationships with everyone else as well.

7. Spiritual Companionship

The Sanskrit word for this is *satsang*: what the Buddha would call "right association," or association with those who are following the same spiritual path. When we are trying to change our life, we need the support of others with the same goal. If you have friends who are meditating along the lines suggested here, it is a great help to meditate together regularly. Share your times of entertainment too; relaxation is an important part of spiritual living.

8. Reading the Mystics

We are so surrounded today by a low concept of what the human being is that it is essential to give ourselves a higher image. For this reason I recommend devoting half an hour or so each day to reading the scriptures and the writings of the great mystics of all religions. Just before bedtime, after evening meditation, is a particularly good time, because the thoughts you fall asleep in will be with you throughout the night.

There is a helpful distinction between works of inspiration and works of spiritual instruction. Inspiration may be drawn from every tradition or religion. Instructions in meditation and other spiritual disciplines, however, can differ from and even seem to contradict each other. For this reason, it is wise to confine instructional reading to the works of one teacher or path. Choose your teacher carefully. A good teacher lives what he or she teaches, and it is the student's responsibility to exercise sound judgment. Then, once you have chosen, give your teacher your full loyalty.

The Way of Love

The Bhagavad Gita, Chapter 12
Translated for use in meditation

ARJUNA:

Of those who love you as the Lord of Love,
Ever present in all, and those who seek you
As the nameless, formless Reality,
Which way is sure and swift, love or knowledge?

SRI KRISHNA:

For those who set their hearts on me
And worship me with unfailing devotion and faith,
The Way of Love leads sure and swift to me.

As for those who seek the transcendental Reality,
Without name, without form,
Contemplating the Unmanifested
Beyond the reach of feeling and of thought,
With their senses subdued and mind serene
And striving for the good of all beings,
They too will verily come unto me.

Yet hazardous and slow is the path to the Unrevealed,
Difficult for physical beings to tread.
But they for whom I am the goal supreme,
Who do all work renouncing self for me
And meditate on me with single-hearted devotion,
These will I swiftly rescue
From the fragment's cycle of birth and death
To fullness of eternal life in me.

Still your mind in me, still yourself in me,
And without doubt you shall be united
With me, Lord of Love, dwelling in your heart.
But if you cannot still your mind in me,
Learn to do so through the practice of meditation.
If you lack the will for such self-discipline,
Engage yourself in selfless service of all around you,
For selfless service can lead you at last to me.
If you are unable to do even this,
Surrender yourself to me in love,
Receiving success and failure with equal calmness
As granted by me.
Better indeed is knowledge than mechanical practice.
Better than knowledge is meditation.
But better still is surrender in love,
Because there follows immediate peace.

A More Ardent Fire

That one I love who is incapable of ill will
And returns love for hatred.
Living beyond the reach of *I* and *mine*
And of pleasure and pain, full of mercy,
Contented, self-controlled, firm in faith,
With all their heart and all their mind given to me –
With such as these I am in love.

Not agitating the world or by it agitated,
They stand above the sway of elation,
Competition, and fear, accepting life
Good and bad as it comes. They are pure,
Efficient, detached, ready to meet every demand
I make on them as humble instruments of my work.

They are dear to me who run not after the pleasant
Nor away from the painful, grieve not
Over the past, lust not today,
But let things come and go as they happen.

Who serve both friend and foe with equal love,
Not buoyed up by praise nor cast down by blame,
Alike in heat and cold, pleasure and pain,
Free from selfish attachments and self-will,
Ever full, in harmony everywhere,

Firm in faith – such as these are dear to me.

But even dearer are those who seek me
In faith and love as life's one supreme goal.
They go beyond death to eternal life.